Crack Your Good Girl Code

Secrets To Reclaiming Your Feminine Power

Joy Balma, MA, MS

Crack Your Good Girl Code is written by Joy Balma

Copyright © 2017, Joy Balma

ISBN 9780991087020

Library of Congress Control Number 2017910194

Brilliant Living Press

www.joybalma.com

Book layout by e-book-design.com

Printed in the USA

Limit of Liability/ Disclaimer of Warranty

The material in this book is intended for education. No expressed or implied guarantee as to the effects of the use of the recommendations can be given nor liability taken. The stories used as examples are based on real experiences. Some of the stories are composites; individual names and identifying detail have been changed. This publication is sold with the understanding that the author is not engaged in rendering psychological, medical or other professional services. If expert assistance is required, the services of a professional should be sought.

Also by Joy Balma

Rock Your Feminine Type To Rock Your Business

Dedication

To my beloved mother who showed me what love is.

Acknowledgments

A special thank you to all the women who read my first book and/or participated in my trainings or coaching programs. Your feedback and stories deepened my understanding of personality types and women's power. Your courage inspired me.

Table of Contents

— THE GOOD GIRL TYPES —

— YOUR SOVEREIGNTY —

Authenticity is the daily practice of letting go of who we think we're supposed to be and embracing who we are.

—Brene Brown

Introduction

As a women's empowerment coach and personality type expert, I have been helping women recognize their patterns, claim their power and unleash their potential for two decades. During this time, I discovered that women can get lost in their accommodating Good Girl and abandon the more powerful aspects of their personality. While the Good Girl in us has many admirable qualities, she has a way of playing small and sabotaging us.

Our feminine power depends on our ability to say *Yes* to ourselves on a deep level. We need to know we are worthy of what we desire and powerful enough to create it. We simply cannot create a life we love if we diminish ourselves, deny our dreams and put our needs last. The Good Girl can find her way into every area of our life and influence all of our relationships, so we need to understand this part of us.

Crack Your Good Girl Code will reboot your Good Girl programming from the ground up. It takes you on a soul-searching journey into the heart of your feminine power where you will recognize how you give your power away. Then, you will discover the tools you need to reclaim your sovereignty.

This is not a self-improvement book, but a book of self-awareness and self-reclamation. It will help you discover and reclaim what has been rightfully yours all along—your worth and power. Through 4 Good Girl Types and 8 Power Plays, your Good Girl patterns will be illuminated and self-sabotage obliterated. You will go from being a damsel in distress to a sovereign queen.

Get ready to crack your Good Girl code.

Joy Balma

Your Wake-Up Call

1

The Good Girl
Within You

Hello Good Girl!

You know who you are!

You struggle to say, "No," agonize about disappointing people and do your best to make sure everyone is happy. You are a nurturer and an accommodator who tries to meet the needs of others, but you often leave yourself out of the picture.

The Good Girl is *The Sweetheart* associated with the archetype of *The Mother*. She embodies unconditional love, compassion and infinite generosity. The Good Girl is a powerful force for healing on the planet with many undeniable virtues. The world would collapse without all her good works. There is no doubt that the Good Girl is phenomenal and deserves our full respect, but this book is about seeing what we don't see about this part of us. You are about to learn more about your Good Girl than you ever thought possible!

Think of all these positive qualities as the front door of your Good Girl's home. We often don't realize that our Good Girl has a back door too. Right alongside her kindness and generosity, she can leave a trail of disempowering patterns.

People-pleasing

Over-giving

Co-dependency

Perfectionism

Inadequate boundary-setting

Failing to speak up

Playing the victim

Ignoring finances

and more

These self-sabotaging patterns can find their way into every area of our life. We can give our power away and not know why. We can play small and not see how. To reclaim our power and live authentically, we need to thoroughly understand how our Good Girl shows up. There is a way in which she can become imbalanced and then significantly limit us. Even if you think of yourself as powerful and confident, I encourage you to read on. You might just find there is a Good Girl in you too.

Hi! I'm Joy and I'm a recovering Good Girl. The funny thing is, I didn't know I had a Good Girl problem. I thought my Good Girl was a saint and a savior all rolled into one! She was my pride and joy. As a women's empowerment coach, I could easily see the disempowering Good Girl patterns of my clients, but I only saw the positive attributes of my own Good Girl. It is when our lives fall apart that we become willing to look at ourselves more closely, and this was the case for me.

After a ten-year relationship with a boyfriend ended, I took some time to observe my contribution. For someone who didn't think they had a Good Girl problem, I was shocked to realize my Good Girl had played the starring role. For ten years I stayed in a relationship where I acted as a rescuer and a fixer to my partner and I wouldn't give up. I was determined to solve his problems, as best I could. The Good Girl doesn't give up on people, no matter what the cost. If she did, she would be a *bad* person!

The Good Girl doesn't give up on people, no matter what the cost.

It became blatantly clear to me that my Good Girl had orchestrated the whole show. In fact, she had the convertible top down, music blaring and was driving me off a cliff. She was behind the wheel of my life and out of control. My Good Girl had thrown all caution to the wind in her rescue mission. It was time to look within. I needed to understand my patterns.

So, like an archeologist digging for clues to an ancient mystery, I began to diligently study my Good Girl patterns. The more I looked, the more I saw. It was like pulling a thread only to realize I was connected to an endless ball of Good Girl yarn. I discovered that I struggled to do what was best for myself, in favor of doing what was best for others—the classic Good Girl dilemma. As I peeled back the layers, I realized my entire life philosophy was a page ripped right out of the Good Girl Handbook which reads:

"Good Girls keep their desires small, put their needs aside— seeking only to give, and never receive. Good Girls don't focus on money. They shrink their needs, so they are not greedy or needy. Most of all, Good Girls are not selfish."

—From *Rock Your Feminine Type To Rock Your Business*

I recognized that my Good Girl prides herself in playing small. Small is good. Small is best. Small is safe. With this revelation, I slammed the brakes on my Good Girl's joyride. We can only change what we see, so I was happy to uncover these disempowering beliefs. One by one, I tossed them out. If we don't keep an eye on our Good Girl, she will jump in our driver's seat and take us on a wild ride.

When our Good Girl is at the wheel of our life, she can ditch our inner Diva. This means we can end up going against our own best interests and instincts. When we ditch our Diva, we abandon our power and even our authentic self. Yep! My Good Girl ditched my Diva! Without the ability to access our inner Diva, we struggle to stay true to ourselves, keep our boundaries or even create a life we really love. When we ditch our Diva, we ditch our power.

When we ditch our Diva, we abandon our power and even our authentic self.

There are infinite ways that we can get stuck wearing a Good Girl mask and not even notice. Women tend to be validated and rewarded for being accommodating Good Girls and not for being powerful. The result is that we often hide our power or give our power away. But don't worry, you are about to crack your Good Girl code. This book will guide you through 4 Good Girl Types and 8 Power Plays. Together, they will help you find the balance between your Good Girl and your Diva. By the end, your Diva will be your new BFF and most powerful ally. You will have the secrets you need to DIVA UP!

Rest assured this process is not about finding fault with your compassionate and caring nature. When we embrace our inner Diva, we are not losing our heart and soul. We are not going to become stingy with our compassion. When we own our Diva's strengths we empower our Good Girl to be effective in the world.

As nurturers, we need to know how to keep our boundaries and stand up for ourselves. We need to know that we can be both good *and* powerful. There is no time to waste. Your Good Girl has the pedal to the metal and she's headed for the cliff. On the other side of this journey is an authentically empowered and awakened woman—you!

How do I know? It happened to me.

2

The Initial Good Girl Assessment

Your power-excavation project starts now. Let's begin by doing an initial assessment of your Good Girl. Put a check by each statement below that describes you:

_____ I struggle to tell people "No."

_____ I am a chronic under-earner.

_____ I don't speak up when I really should.

_____ I help others with their dreams and abandon my own.

_____ I avoid money matters.

_____ I don't call people out on their bad behavior.

_____ I don't like to create boundaries, so I don't.

_____ I feel responsible for everyone's happiness.

_____ I am terrified of being judged as less than perfect.

_____ I take great pride in being generous and selfless.

_____ I often feel unappreciated for all that I do for others.

_____ I go to great lengths to avoid disappointing people.

_____ I am a people-pleaser.

_____ I rely on other people to validate and approve of me.

_____ I have been known to rescue people.

_____ Total Good Girl Score

Score Total 1 - 5

Your Good Girl is **OUT OF BALANCE**

**You are leaving
yourself out of your own life.**

Score Total 6 – 10

Your Good Girl has **TAKEN OVER**

Burnout is around the corner.

Score Total 11 – 15

Your Good Girl has **DITCHED YOUR DIVA**

You are ready for a Good Girl rebellion.

You may have put a check mark on every statement for a total score of 15. Or, you might have looked at the Good Girl assessment and thought, "None of these statements represent me!" It is important to know that even wise and confident women have a Good Girl in them.

The Good Girl is not a one size fits all. She has many layers and levels. My Good Girl is not exactly the same as your Good Girl. There is the Good Girl who plays small and another who is determined to be her best. Her idea of being a Good Girl is to be an achiever.

In Chapter 9, you will have the chance to discover your exact Good Girl Type. When you know your Type, you will understand how your Good Girl creates self-abandoning and self-sabotaging patterns in your life. And, you will also know what to do about it. But don't jump ahead or you will miss all the secrets you need to reclaim your power and crack your Good Girl code.

Are you ready?

Let's look at Power Play #1.

3

Power Play #1

Uncover the Good Girl Rules

The first Power Play is to uncover the Good Girl Rules. We need to understand her cherished virtues and values. Let's take a look at them.

The Good Girl Rules

Give more than you receive

Be humble and selfless

Put the needs of others before your own

Don't be bossy, bitchy, controlling or pushy

Don't be greedy or focus on money

These Rules may not seem to be a problem at first glance, but our Good Girl reinterprets their meaning:

"Give more than you receive," becomes
"I don't have needs and desires"

"Be humble and selfless," becomes
"I am not important."

"Put the needs of others before your own," becomes
"I don't matter"

"Don't be bossy, bitchy, controlling or pushy," becomes
"I shouldn't speak up."

"Don't be greedy or focus on money," becomes
"Money is not important and I shouldn't be prosperous."

These interpretations create a layer of hidden messages that we unconsciously live out.

The Good Girl's Hidden Messages

I don't have needs and desires

I am not important

I don't matter

I shouldn't speak up

Money is not important

I shouldn't be prosperous

We often can't see our Good Girl's core beliefs, and yet they drive our life. Looking at this list above, you can see how it is possible to become an expert in self-doubt, self-denial, self-sacrifice and even self-sabotage! The Good Girl thinks she is being virtuous when she plays small—the smaller she makes herself, the better. These certainly aren't the values we signed up for at the Good Girl Club. Being a Good Girl looked rosy at the front door. But from the back door, our highest virtues and values can turn into a virus of powerlessness.

All of this happens below the surface of our awareness. The most empowering thing we can do is unearth our Good Girl's hidden beliefs, and this book will guide you step-by-step.

The Good Girl thinks she is being
virtuous when she plays small—the
smaller she makes herself, the better.

— The Good Girl Box —

The Good Girl learns to downplay her value, and herself. She doesn't want to take up too much space or expand too boldly. So, like a squirrel who hides its treasure in a million secret places, the Good Girl hides her treasure too—her power.

She never wants to be judged as aggressive, selfish or controlling because this goes against the Good Girl Rules. To avoid this, she climbs into a safe space of acceptable behavior—the Good Girl Box. Little by little, she gives up parts of herself in order to fit snugly into the small container. She wants to be liked, accepted and validated. Over time, the Good Girl becomes adept at subtly changing herself to please others. She learns to be what others want her to be in order to receive their approval, acceptance and love.

The Good Girl learns to be what others
want her to be in order to receive
approval, acceptance and love.

Even strong-willed and ambitious women get shoved into the Good Girl Box. They are shamed for their strength, chastised for being *too much*, and bullied for being *too bold*. They are admonished that they should be more demure and ladylike. No woman should live her life in a Good Girl Box waiting for the approval and validation of others, but we often do. There are many ways we can get stuck there.

It's time for an evolution revolution—to expand beyond your Good Girl Box so you can know yourself in a whole new way. Maybe you are ready to break loose, or maybe you are not even aware of your Good Girl. Either way, you are about to learn what is on the other side—your authentically empowered self.

4

Power Play #2

Own Your Worth

It's not your job to like me, it's mine.

—Byron Katie

To live from a place of sovereignty, you need to know that your *worth* is non-negotiable. When you own your worth, you act powerfully. You make decisions based on what is best for you, instead of giving your power away to others through people-pleasing. Our worth and power go hand-in-hand. If we don't feel worthy, we won't feel deserving of abundance, success or even the fulfillment of our dreams.

Power Play #2
Own Your Worth

Think of your worth as your throne. It is important to sit in your own seat of authority and own it like a queen! And yet, it isn't so easy to own our worth. It often feels more acceptable to judge and criticize ourselves. Think of how hard it is, sometimes, to simply accept a compliment. We often won't let ourselves feel that we are *good enough*, because that might mean we are self-centered. Anything that resembles selfishness is banished by our Good Girl—she translates self-love to mean that she is selfish.

One thing is for sure, everyone is happy to tell us who they think we *should* be in order to be worthy. We are besieged with societal judgments, gender expectations and media ideals telling us we need to:

Be thin, but not too thin

Be smart, but not too smart

Be sexy, but not too sexy

Be attractive, but not attention-grabbing

Be successful, but not too successful

Be powerful, but not domineering

Be competent, but not controlling.

Make money, but don't be greedy.

The list is endless.

Mixed messages can bury us alive under an avalanche of insecurity and inadequacy. If we don't follow these ever-changing dictates, we fear we will not be worthy, happy, loved or accepted. We can become contortionists, twisting and turning ourselves into pretzel-like shapes to fulfill the needs of others.

As young girls, we learn to be what others want us to be. We are convinced that our worth is in what other's think of us. So, we modify how we appear by changing our hair, clothes, bodies and even our mind-set in any given situation.

We are convinced that our worth is in what others think of us.

Alas, we can never win at this game. Even after jumping through all these hoops, we are still judged as either *not good enough*, or as *too much*. In response to all this criticism and judgment, we can fall into a Good Girl coma, become self-improvement junkies, or just give up on ourselves. These roads are filled with addictions, depression, and obsessions that promise to fill the void in our self-worth, but never do.

It is only natural and human to want to be accepted, loved and valued. But it is not wise to change ourselves for others, or to rely on them to establish our value. If we do, we give them our power.

It's tempting to blame others for our lack of self-worth. It is easy to create a scapegoat such as our parents, partner, boss, children, friends, family members or someone else. But we are empowered to the extent that we take full responsibility for our value, and our life. If we blame others, we will remain stuck.

When we let others define our value, we fall down the slippery slope of disempowerment. No one can give us our self-worth or take it away. We won't find our value through the validation of others, or even by creating perfect circumstances. The whole world can adore you, but if all you see are your flaws you will never be happy. You are the only one who can determine your worth. This is both your privilege and your responsibility.

> If you rely on people to establish your value, you give them your power.

You are the only one who
can determine your worth.
This is both your privilege
and your responsibility.

Your Awakening

5

Power Play #3

Discover Your Diva

I don't follow the rules. I never did and I'm not going to start.

—Madonna

When you stop trying to please everyone to earn their approval, you begin the journey to truly know yourself. Dormant parts of you begin to stir. Just as you have an inner Good Girl, you also have an inner Diva. She is the counterpart and the counterbalance to your Good Girl. The role she plays is part rebel, part wise priestess and part fairy godmother. She is your resident sovereign queen.

Power Play #3 is
Discover Your Diva

You have heard the voice of your inner Diva over the course of your life. Sometimes she whispers, and other times she shouts to get your attention. She says:

Trust your gut

You are enough

Follow your heart

Do what is best for yourself

Discover who you really are

Speak up and tell your truth

Don't worry about fitting in

We often choose jobs, partners and lifestyles based on our Good Girl's desire to do what is *right*, to be *good* and to fit in. Our Diva, on the other hand, asks us what we really want and guides us to stay true to ourselves. She is a breath of fresh air.

Our Diva asks us what we really want and guides us to stay true to ourselves.

What is your reaction to the word Diva? Do you envision a self-centered woman making outrageous demands of others like a pampered princess? Or, maybe you think a Diva is a cold woman? The word Diva could have a positive connotation for you, such as queen.

Diva literally means *Goddess* in Italian. In comes from the Latin word *Diva* which is the feminine of *Divus* or Divine, God. In this book, Diva represents your authentically empowered self—the part of you who knows your value and wouldn't dream of betraying it.

Your inner Diva does not have the spoiled Princess Complex where she demands that people attend to her exhaustive list of needs and desires. A woman with the Princess Complex is not confident—she is a damsel in distress. Our Diva, on the other hand, is our worthy inner queen.

Our Diva is our worthy inner queen.

Imagine standing in your value without apologizing for your flaws. Your Diva gives you the courage to face your fears, move through challenges and accomplish your goals. Discovering my Diva was the missing link to reclaiming my power. She gave me a life-saving infusion of positive self-esteem and healthy self-centeredness. This was precisely the elixir I needed to restore my Good Girl's power.

When you know how to access your inner Diva, it is like stepping into her red stilettos. Perhaps you are ready to kick off your goodie-two-shoes! When you wear her red heels, your goals feel attainable instead of as a distant dream. Excuses fade and you get to work creating a life you are excited about—one that does not include playing small or giving your power away!

Your Diva helps you:

Dream bigger	Live unapologetically
Know your purpose	Accomplish your goals
Celebrate your real self	Receive from others
Share your gifts	Celebrate your successes
Guard your time	Know that you are enough
Come out of hiding	Stay focused on your goals
Believe in yourself	Speak up and tell your truth
Follow your heart	Embrace & enjoy pleasure
Honor your feelings	Be self-expressive
Trust your intuition	Decide what is best for you
Create financial flow	Accept & express your power
Face challenges	Create and keep boundaries
Own your sexuality	Say "No" or "Yes" as you wish
Be your authentic self	Embrace and attract money
Live by your own rules	Step into a leadership role

This list represents tremendous power—your power! You don't want to miss out on all your radiant Diva energy! It's time to let your Diva out of her genie bottle, so she can work her magic in your life.

Let your Diva out of her genie bottle,
so she can work her magic in your life.

Looking at the list above, pick one statement that resonates strongly with you and turn it into your new power mantra. Such as "I celebrate my successes." Or, "I know that I am enough." You can come back later and refresh your power mantra by choosing a new one.

My Power Mantra Is:

Power! You have it, you just need to claim it. This is not power over others, or power to control others. As well, this is not a masculine energy. Your Diva is your deep feminine—your inner priestess, goddess and sovereign queen. She provides you with the knowledge of your worth and power and connects you to your authentic self. It's time to befriend her.

Your inner Diva will help you take off your Good Girl mask and celebrate who you really are. A woman is powerful to the extent that she knows her authentic self and is willing to stand up for it. Living as a cookie-cutter version of someone else does not lead to a life you love. You are a one-of-a-kind combination of personality traits. There is nothing more empowering than being your true self and being true to yourself. This is your life. Make it your own.

A woman is powerful to
the extent that she knows
her authentic self and
is willing to stand up for it.

6

Has Your Good Girl
Ditched Your Diva?

You are not built to shrink down to less but blossom into more.

—Oprah Winfrey

While all this sounds exciting, often the last thing your Good Girl wants to be is a Diva! She fears being seen as bossy, selfish or demanding, so your Good Girl takes over your life. She hops into your driver's seat and peels out leaving your Diva by the side of the road holding a suitcase full of your power. That's right! Your precious Good Girl ditches your Diva.

Why does she do this? How does she do this? We need to know.

— The Good Girl/Bad Girl Trap —

When we set out to live our lives fully and powerfully, we can get caught between polarized stereotypes of the Good Girl and the Bad Girl. We unconsciously feel forced to choose between the two. Are we the Good Girl who is kind, but gives her power away? Or, are we the Bad Girl who is powerful, but intimidating?

**Are we the Good Girl who is kind,
but gives her power away?**

Or

**Are we the Bad Girl who is powerful,
but intimidating?**

Society puts the Good Girl on a pedestal, while the Bad Girl is rejected and reprimanded. Merely the thought of being judged as a Bad Girl can cause us to give our power away. For example, we can be judged harshly for simply speaking our mind and taking a stand. In response, we may run back to our Good Girl Box and close the lid. From our Good Girl Box, we don't speak up or call people out on their bad behavior. We don't stand our ground or stand up for ourselves. Instead, we are overly polite. In fact, we can even back down and then apologize for making trouble! The Good Girl hates to be a bother to anyone.

The line between Good Girl and Bad Girl shifts, so we never quite know when we might be shamed for stepping outside the Good Girl circle. For example, one minute we are rewarded for being attractive, and in the next we are shamed for being too attractive.

No one likes to be judged or limited, but if we step outside our Good Girl Box we need to be ready for this possibility. When we stand in our power, we can trigger judgment from others. This is why your Good Girl ditches your Diva. She is afraid she will be judged as the Bad Girl.

When we stand in our power, we can trigger judgment from others.

Women can be judged as Bad Girls for simply being themselves— for having their own thoughts, ambitions, feelings, opinions, needs, dreams, desires, sexuality, point of view and creative self-expression. When we welcome our inner Diva into our personality, we own these lost and forgotten parts of our self instead of denying them to suit the needs of others. When we access our inner Diva, we no longer:

- *Abandon ourselves in order to please others.*

- *Apologize for doing what is right for us.*

- *Give up our power in order to get the approval of others.*

- *Hide our authentic self.*

- *Downplay our value, play small or hide.*

It's up to us to see through the Good Girl/Bad Girl trap, so we can access both our authenticity and our feminine power. It would be nice if we could control the opinions of others. But no matter how accommodating we are, people will always judge. When you DIVA UP, you are not becoming a cruel and uncaring person. You are merely giving yourself permission to be yourself. You never have to apologize for being yourself.

— The Sacred Balance —

A little more kick-ass and a little less kiss-ass is necessary to reboot your Good Girl programming. The truth is, if your Good Girl is out of balance, she will sabotage all your best efforts. She influences your relationship magnetism, your money mojo and your leadership moxie. Finding the balance between our Good Girl and our Diva is a sacred tightrope we walk as women.

On one side, our Good Girl asks,

"What do others need from me? How can I help?"

On the other side, our Diva asks,

"What is true for me? What do I need to do
to take care of myself?"

This balancing act is the key to creating a life you love and a life that works for you. Our feminine power blooms when we equally accept and express both our Good Girl and our Diva.

Our authentic power blooms when
we equally accept and express
both our Good Girl and our Diva.

The Good Girl in us is a giver. Her natural impulse is to attend to the needs of others and abandon herself. Relationships need a certain amount of selflessness, compromise and negotiation. But the Good Girl doesn't know where to draw the line between selflessness that is necessary and selflessness that is self-abandonment. With our Diva by our side, we know exactly where to draw this line.

> ## The Good Girl doesn't know where to draw the line between selflessness that is *necessary* and selflessness that is *self-abandonment*.

— Does This Really Work For Me? —

The Good Girl mind-set has deep roots in us. Being accommodating, dutiful and compliant used to be necessary for our survival, and in many parts of the world it still is. We fight for the freedoms we have. If we don't, we get stuck in the Good Girl Box. The problem is, we can act like butterflies caught in a jar. Even if the lid is no longer there, we sometimes don't fly out. On a deep level, we can be confused about our right to do so, and conflicted about what it means to be a powerful woman. One thing is for sure, we need to give ourselves permission to do what is best for ourselves.

To find this essential balance in any situation, ask yourself this question, *"Does this really work for me?"* If the answer is *"No,"* then you need to honor your truth. Your truth may not always please people. Honor it anyway. Look back to the times in your life when you wished you had sincerely asked yourself this question, and been able to answer it with your best interest at heart.

Your truth may not
always please people.
Honor it anyway.

A Tour of the Good Girl Galaxy

I want every girl who is told she is bossy, to be told instead she has leadership skills.

—Sheryl Sandberg

Hop on the Good Girl bus and let's take a tour. There are six clues that tell you that your Good Girl has ditched your Diva:

6 Clues Your Good Girl Has Ditched Your Diva

Being Overly Nice

Ignoring Intuition

Over-Apologizing

Believing "I don't matter"

Using Good Girl Language

Abandoning Leadership

— Being Overly Nice —

The Good Girl struggles to find her balance between telling her truth and pleasing people. Her fear is that she will push people away if she says what is true for her. She also wants to be liked, so she tells people what they want to hear. In doing so, she falls into a trap where she can't keep her boundaries or even say "No."

Being overly nice is Good Girl crack. It's her addiction. She only wants to be seen as positive, nurturing and agreeable, so she sacrifices her truth and her authenticity. The result is a continual cycle of self-betrayal and self-abandonment. Being nice is important, but so is being truthful. The kindest thing we can do is to tell our truth, even if it may be difficult.

The kindest thing we can do is to tell our truth, even if it may be difficult.

On a day-to-day basis, we need to speak up so we can keep our boundaries. If we don't, we pay a big price. The price is burnout, anger, resentment and more.

On a larger scale, imagine if women never told their truth. We would all be huddled in our Good Girl Boxes and the whole world would suffer. Sometimes we have to become a fighter to stand up for what is right, or a warrior to fight for what is true, or a rebel in order to preserve what is good. It is important to know when our boundaries have been crossed and speak up. Being a good person includes standing up for things that matter.

Just as power is taboo for women, so is the expression of anger and aggression. This means we can become complacent and fail to keep our boundaries. It is valid to be angry when we see injustice or experience it. Sitting on the sidelines of life because our opinions or feelings might offend someone is dangerous. It is time to expand our definition and expression of feminine power beyond the realm of simply being nice. When a woman is authentic, she knows when to be a warrior, a rebel or a fighter. She doesn't relegate herself to her Good Girl Box. She doesn't turn a blind-eye to injustice.

Feminine power is more than just getting the Miss Congeniality award. There are many shades of feminine power that we need to discover, accept, express and celebrate. This is how we evolve. We shortchange ourselves if we get stuck on "nice" like a broken record and never show up fully.

Feminine power is more than just getting the Miss Congeniality award.

— Ignoring Intuition —

Imagine having a superpower that you never use. This is how we often treat our feminine superpower of intuition. The Good Girl doesn't want to know the truth, because then she would have to deal with what she knows. It is more comfortable to pretend she doesn't see certain things. In order to do this, she disconnects from her inner knowing—her intuition.

This may not appear to have any consequences, but it does. If we have a bad feeling about a person or a situation, it is vital to pay attention. Our intuition is our built-in alarm system. It guides us to opportunities and saves us from negative people and situations. It also helps us in practical ways. Our intuition is our own internal guidance system (IGS.)

One day, I was putting gas in my car to go to an event that was a two-hour drive away. As I was waiting for the gas tank to fill, I had this overwhelming feeling that I shouldn't make the trip. The feeling was clear as a bell—"Don't go!" I had been excited to attend this event, so I was confused. Our intuition is often confusing because it goes against our rational mind, but I knew better than to ignore my IGS. I had a lot of experience ignoring these internal cues, and I wasn't about to do it again! I decided to go home, and I found out the event had been cancelled. My intuition saved me from a four-hour road trip.

While our Good Girl turns off her intuition so she can be nice, our Diva cranks up the volume. She is all ears! If we give up our connection to our intuition, we give up on our connection to the truth. We need to power up our inner knowing instead of turning it off. It could save our life.

To take advantage of your intuition superpower, start by paying attention. Overtime, you become an expert in recognizing and trusting your IGS.

> While our Good Girl turns off her
> intuition so she can be nice,
> our Diva cranks up the volume.

— Over-Apologizing —

Apologizing is a healing balm. A sincere, "I'm sorry" is magic. Relationships cannot survive and thrive if we don't take responsibility for our actions and apologize when necessary. There is nothing better than getting an apology from someone when it is needed and deserved, but over-apologizing is different. Over-apologizing is when we take all the blame and let the other person off the hook.

The Good Girl over-apologizes in order to:

- *Be liked and accepted*

- *Assuage the anger of others*

- *Avoid a disagreement or difficult conversation*

There is a place for apologizing and acknowledging wrong-doing, but taking all the blame can create an imbalance in our relationships. On an everyday basis the Good Girl wants to convey the message that she is a nice person, so she gets into the habit of over-apologizing. She apologizes for taking up space and speaking up, and this ends up being a way to play small. When we over-apologize, we are really saying, "I don't matter" or "I am nice."

Of course, if you're late for an appointment and you've kept people waiting, you owe them an apology. If you spill a drink on your friend's carpet, offer a sincere "I'm so sorry." If you bump into someone, say "Excuse me," but you don't need to apologize for everyday acts of speaking up and taking up space. You are important. You matter. In fact, take up some more room and suck up some more air. To create a life you love, don't apologize for doing what is right for you. Live unapologetically.

To create a life you love, don't apologize for doing what is right for you. Live unapologetically.

— Believing "I don't matter" —

Over-apologizing is one of the many ways the Good Girl expresses her hidden belief, "I don't matter." You can imagine the damage this one thought can have. It can lead to all kinds of self-sabotaging behaviors such as:

- *Over-eating*
- *Eating poorly*
- *Over-spending*
- *Not speaking up*
- *Being sedentary*
- *Not saying, "No"*
- *Not valuing your time*
- *Not keeping boundaries*
- *Giving up on your goals*
- *Remaining in abusive or unfulfilling relationships*
- *Staying in careers and jobs you dislike*
- *Remaining broke*

Because of the hidden belief, "I don't matter," the Good Girl can struggle to take positive action on her own behalf. She, instead, suffers in silence and stuffs her feelings. Her own needs always come last, if ever. She invests all her energy in making sure everyone around her is happy, while her needs end up going underground.

Ashley loved being single. She was divorced and decided that having a few boyfriends worked for her. She liked all the attention. She often juggled two and sometimes three regular relationships. They all claimed to be in love with her. They enjoyed common interests by attending concerts and events, and she was intimate with all of them. Ashley was convinced that this was enough for her. She wanted their love and companionship and didn't want to push them away by making demands. It all worked because she didn't ask anything of them.

Everything was fine until Ashley got sick and her boyfriends went off to find greener pastures. Ashley was left alone with some time to think. It didn't feel good to be dumped when she really needed help. She thought they loved her. It sank in that she had been fooling herself.

She spent many nights crying over the realization that she didn't feel worthy enough to ask for a real relationship. She had been investing in relationships of convenience, but she was worth more than that. She now knew she wanted and deserved more.

Ashley made a commitment to find a real life partner who was willing to go the distance with her, and she wasn't going to settle for less.

Making sure everyone around you is happy, but leaving yourself out of the picture is a signature Good Girl move. It's a way of saying, "I don't matter." Reducing our needs and playing small may seem to be a good idea, but it doesn't help us create the life we want. Dare to expand into your worth and power instead of shrinking.

Dare to expand into your worth and power instead of shrinking.

— Using Good Girl Language —

Our words reveal what we truly believe. In fact, our language expresses our entire world view. Imagine you are sharing your goals with a friend and you say, "My *little* plan is... I *kind of* want to... It's *just* an idea... I *hope* I can..."

"Kind of"
"Little"
"Just"
"I hope"

You might be shocked to realize how often you use these phrases to diminish yourself and negate what you are saying. Pay particular attention to the word "little," and eliminate it from your vocabulary. Adopt a vocabulary of power. You can start by owning the word *Diva* to reflect a woman who knows her value. Words are the wings of your beliefs. They both reflect your reality and create it.

— Abandoning Leadership —

Leadership brings us face-to-face with our power issues. Whether you need to be the leader of your business, in your family or as an employee, it is essential to understand how your Good Girl is showing up. Becoming an effective and successful leader is often the missing link for the heart-centered Good Girl.

Leadership brings us face-to-face with our power issues.

When your Good Girl is out of balance, she can struggle with:

- *Delegation*

- *Boundary setting*

- *Saying, "No"*

- *Perfectionism*

- *Money*

- *Communication*

- *Ambition*

- *Over-giving/Discounting*

- *Promoting, selling and visibility*

When we bring our Diva out of the shadows, we bring our leader out of the shadows. We stop being dreamers and become doers. We stop being pleasers and become the CEO of our life. And, we stop shrinking ourselves to meet the needs of others.

When we bring our Diva out of the shadows, we bring our leader out of the shadows too.

With your Diva on board, you can play a whole new leadership game. You can:

- *Say "No"*

- *Close the sale*

- *Be decisive*

- *Follow your intuition*

- *Stand in your spotlight*

- *Accomplish your goals*

- *Focus on making money*

- *Move through obstacles*

- *Communicate effectively*

- *Own your worth and power*

- *Hire and fire appropriately*

- *Build visibility and influence*

- *Change course as necessary*

- *Create and keep boundaries*

- *Own your ambition and desires*

- *Promote and sell without apology*

Your power and effectiveness in the world depends on your ability to breakthrough any barrier you have placed in your own way. This requires building new pathways of thinking and taking new actions. Embracing your inner Diva doesn't mean you won't experience self-doubt, anxiety or indecision. You are not expected to jump from being a humble Good Girl to being a fearless Diva, nor is this the goal. You become empowered when you find the balance between your Good Girl and your Diva and neither part of you is left behind.

You become empowered when
you find the balance between
your Good Girl & your Diva.

— Let's Get Visible —

In order to be an effective leader, start by putting visibility at the top of your list. You don't have to be a gifted promoter, but you do need to come out of hiding. You need visibility to build influence. It is not vain to be proud of your talents and to let people know about them. If you opt out of visibility, you opt out of influence which includes financial success.

> If you opt out of visibility, you opt out of influence which includes financial success.

You can be an expert in your field, but if you are invisible you can't help people with your knowledge. You may be a heart-centered healer, but if you aren't willing to be seen you can't help as many people as you would like. You may be a creative genius, but if no one sees your work you can't share your insights and ideas.

Loosen your grip on all your excuses and explore new ways of expressing yourself. If you act the same old way, you will get the same old results. Once you try on your Diva's style and give it a whirl, you just might find that you like standing in her shoes. It feels good to own your worth and power—very good!

For most women, their Good Girl has been in charge for a long time. Stepping outside the warm and cozy Good Girl comfort zone is not easy. Showing up in a whole new way is both exhilarating and terrifying. When you make changes, the people in your life will need to make adjustments too—they will have to grow and evolve along with you. There will be growing pains when you get in touch with your inner Diva, but your freedom and authenticity are worth it. You are worth it.

Tell the truth
Trust your intuition
Apologize appropriately
Use a language of power
Know that you matter
Step into leadership

8

Make Your Diva Your New BFF

*The quality of strength lined with tenderness
is an unbeatable combination.*

—Maya Angelou

Your Diva is your wise inner priestess and authentic voice. Her power, wisdom and sovereignty do not make her cruel, vain or selfish. Surprise! Your Diva is actually your fairy godmother full of moxie and magic. She gives you permission to be yourself and to be true to yourself.

Your Diva isn't a Bad Girl.
She is your fairy godmother.

Your inner Diva is also a creatrix. She is the part of you who gets things done because she knows how to harness her creative power. She is a possibility thinker in tune with her ambitions and desires. When you make your Diva an integral part of your personality, you won't sit on the sidelines asking for permission to take the lead in your life. You won't put your life on hold waiting until you feel that you are perfect enough, good enough or smart enough. You realize that you don't have to take a backseat to your dreams, or to anyone else. Instead, you will speak up, step up and shine.

Power Play #4
Make Your Diva Your New BFF

Imagine being able to effortlessly say "No" to projects and requests that are just not your priority. When your Good Girl and your Diva work together, you have this ability. You become a tour de force. You move through the world unapologetically and courageously. You know how to be kind and generous without down playing your value or being a victim—this is feminine power.

You know how to be kind and generous
without down playing your value or
being a victim—this is feminine power.

The good news is that your Diva is right where you are—inside you. She is just waiting for you to welcome her, and respect her. She is there for you!

— Nurturing Love and Tough Love —

Think of your Good Girl as nurturing love and your Diva as tough love. They are on the same team—"Team You!" When they work together, you win. You can create your life in a way that honors your authentic self. Everything you do reflects your worth and power. Just like a mother needs both nurturing love and tough love to raise wise, kind and powerful children, we need both of these aspects for ourselves as well.

When you welcome your Diva, a whole new world opens up to you. Dreams you had given up on now seem attainable. You become a possibility thinker. Your Diva helps you own your worth, find your passion and harness your power—no more playing small, thinking small or believing you are small. That game is over! No matter what mountain you are scaling or what valley you are crawling out of, befriending your Diva takes you to new empowering heights.

Without your truth-telling Diva, your play-by-the-rules Good Girl retreats to be safe. Don't worry though, you are learning how to DIVA UP! You are already discovering that there is no point in diminishing your value or down playing your potential. There is no reason to ditch your Diva! When your Diva is your new BFF, it's like getting an automatic upgrade to first class! Accept the benefits and enjoy the ride. You're going places.

Your Diva helps you access:

Your Joy	*Your Needs*
Your Truth	*Your True Feelings*
Your Voice	*Your Freedom*
Your Worth	*Your Pleasure*
Your Power	*Your Sexuality*
Your Ambition	*Your Happiness*
Your Dreams	*Your Self-Expression*
Your Intuition	*Your Authentic Self*

— Rebellion Is Good for the Soul —

Escaping our Good Girl Box does not mean we leave behind our compassionate, kind and caring nature. It means we include our Diva—our power and our sovereignty. But in order to do this, we need to stake a claim for our truth and freedom. This includes rebelling against anything that limits us, and identifying the ways in which we limit ourselves. Rebellion is good for the soul. It is the key to our feminine sovereignty. When we rebel, we say, "No, this doesn't work for me and I am making a change."

Rebellion is good for the soul. It is the key to our feminine sovereignty.

To do this, you need to come face-to-face with the reasons (excuses) you use to keep yourself limited. What are your excuses for not stepping into your power? How do you hold yourself back? Make a list. The truth is, you can't rule your queendom and nurse excuses. You have to make a choice. Are you going to sit on your excuses like a mother hen, or sit on your throne of power?

— What Would My Diva Do? —

If you feel stuck, tap into your Diva's wisdom. She will always tell you the truth—your truth. I created a guided imagery process to help you connect with your inner Diva. You will hear client examples throughout this book. You can connect with this part of yourself through journaling, guided imagery or even play-acting. Think of an area of your life that needs a Diva makeover. All your Good Girl tricks have failed to create the magic you want. It's impossible to make headway if you play small, think small and act small.

Find a journal and some colored markers. Draw a picture of your Diva. Write some words to describe her and give her a name. Take your time and have fun with this. Then, write down your question for your Diva. The secret is to answer the question with your non-dominant hand. Your writing might be sloppy, and it may feel uncomfortable, but don't worry about that.

You could also go into your closet to find your most glorious Goddess inspired outfit and become your Diva. Embody her to the best of your ability. Bring your inner actress out to play your Diva. Step into your majesty. Maybe your Diva has a totally different voice than yours or an exotic accent! Who doesn't like to play dress up? Now is your chance. Have fun channeling the incredible energy of your Diva. Let your Diva answer your question in her own voice and unique style.

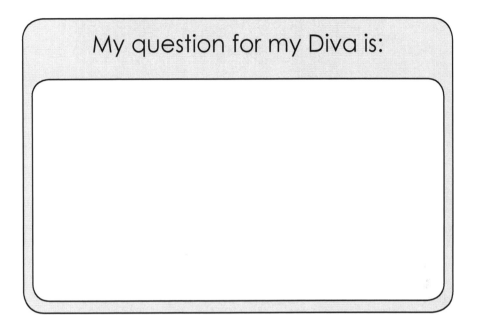

Hello Diva,

(use the name you gave her above)

How am I giving my power away in this situation?

What are my reasons for playing small?

What can I do to reclaim my power?

What is the truth of my worth?

How can I show up powerfully in this situation?

What is my next step?

The Good Girl Types

9

The Good Girl Questionnaire

Now it's time to zero in on your specific Good Girl Type. When you know your Type, you will no longer act out your Good Girl programming unconsciously. Instead, you will have a choice in how you respond to life.

When answering the following questions, keep a few things in mind. The reality is that we can be different people in different situations. For example, you may speak up loud and clear in your personal life, but avoid difficult conversations in your work environment. In this case, you want to claim that pattern and give it at least 1 point.

Or, you might read a statement and think, "I don't do 'that' anymore." But if you just broke that pattern a short time ago, do not dismiss it. The statement reflects a pattern you have, so give it at least 1 point.

Score the statements with the following points:

3 points – Yes, this is true for me

1 point – This is rarely true for me

0 points – This is never true for me

_____ I struggle to create or enforce boundaries.

_____ I keep my feelings, needs and opinions to myself.

_____ I don't speak up when I really need to.

_____ I avoid difficult conversations. I don't have them.

_____ I go to great lengths to avoid disappointing people.

_____ People have taken advantage of my silence.

_____ **Total for Group 1**

_____ I am a people-pleaser.

_____ I let others take the lead and sometimes take over.

_____ I am out of touch with my own goals and dreams.

_____ I easily give up on myself.

_____ I struggle with debilitating self-doubt.

_____ I agonize over saying "No" to people.

_____ **Total for Group 2**

_____ I have been known to rescue and even try to fix people.

_____ I avoid talking about money.

_____ I never give up on people, no matter what the cost.

_____ I like to give, but I have trouble receiving.

_____ I take great pride in being selfless and generous.

_____ People have taken advantage of my generosity.

_____ **Total for Group 3**

_____ My high standards are not optional for me.

_____ The harder I work the more important I feel.

_____ I believe there is a *right* way to do everything.

_____ I put on a show, so people think I am perfect.

_____ I am terrified of being judged as less than perfect.

_____ I work very hard but I never feel I am *good enough*

_____ **Total for Group 4**

Write your total score for each group:

Group 1 _____ The Peacekeeper

Group 2 _____ The Pleaser

Group 3 _____ The Fixer

Group 4 _____ The Perfectionist

My Good Girl Type is:

_____ / _____

Example: The Peacekeeper / Fixer

More than likely, your personality incorporates aspects of all these Good Girl Types to some degree. Your two highest group scores represent your Good Girl Type. Your Good Girl personality has both positive aspects and negative aspects—a front door and a back door. If you don't know your Good Girl Type, it acts like quicksand stealing your potential and your power right out from under you! Don't worry, you are about to be thrown a lifeline as you learn all about your Good Girl personality.

Let's look at the 4 Good Girl Types: **the Peacekeeper, the Pleaser, the Fixer and the Perfectionist.**

The Peacekeeper

Virtue: *Harmony*

Hidden Belief: *I am worthy if I am nice*

The Peacekeeper keeps things light, easy and breezy. She represents the virtue of harmony. She has the ability to smooth the tension right out of the room. She wouldn't dream of creating drama or stirring up trouble. At her best, she brings a powerful stillness and thoughtful presence to everything she does. She can see all sides of a situation and helps people to find common ground.

Things get complicated though when we don't speak up to share our own feelings, thoughts, needs and opinions for fear of creating conflict. The Peacekeeper has a long list of reasons why she withholds her own point of view—all she has to do is pick one of them:

- *She doesn't want to bother anyone.*

- *She believes it is virtuous to avoid conflict.*

- *She wants to avoid creating a disagreement or argument.*

- *She doesn't want to have to stand her ground.*

- *She doesn't feel safe expressing her point of view.*

- *She only wants to be seen as a nice person.*

- *She is not comfortable with uncomfortable emotions.*

- *She fears people will not respect her views.*

The Peacekeeper may not be your *primary* Good Girl type, but unless you know how to deal with conflict, there is probably a part of you who is a Peacekeeper too. Women struggle to have their voices heard, so it is important to understand the Peacekeeper's dilemma.

Keeping the peace is a great idea. Wanting people to be happy is important, but relationships require dialogue and truth-telling.

Without discussion, it is impossible to develop mature relationships where everyone is seen and heard.

Because the Peacekeeper doesn't speak up, she has no chance of getting her needs met or of contributing her point of view. Instead, she lets things ride, accepts pat answers and sweeps things under the rug. She is an expert at stuffing her own needs, feelings and opinions. The end result is that misunderstandings abound, boundaries are crossed and feelings are hurt.

Now the Peacekeeper has another dilemma. She is aware that her boundaries have been crossed, but she still doesn't want to share her feelings. Confrontation and disagreements go against her Good Girl code of ethics, so she turns a blind-eye again. She never wants to be seen as anything but nice, and this is how she gives away her power. She can't tell her truth because she doesn't want to appear pushy, angry, mean or disagreeable.

> She can't tell her truth because she
> doesn't want to appear pushy,
> angry, mean or disagreeable.

Confrontation = Death for the Peacekeeper, so she runs from it. If a conflict develops, she will try to find a resolution as soon as possible, even if it means betraying herself. She fiercely protects her Good Girl image. She often does this by pretending that things don't bother her. Remaining silent can be very powerful. There is great wisdom in being serene and non-reactive. But there are times when being silent means we are giving our power away! The Peacekeeper needs to know the difference.

It would be nice if people naturally respected each other's boundaries. The Peacekeeper believes that people should know the *right* thing to do without her having to tell them. But people aren't mind readers. Relationships need direct communication. If The Peacekeeper doesn't speak up, she can be overlooked and even devalued by others.

Abby was a soft-spoken woman who was frustrated with the people in her work environment. She told me that they disrespected her.

When Abby spoke with her coworkers, she presented a calm, shy demeanor. Her coworkers knew she didn't maintain her boundaries, so she was pegged as the office scapegoat. They blamed her for everything because she was an easy target. Abby was distraught about this, but she didn't know what to do to change the situation.

Every day, her workplace was a tumultuous experience, and she was ready to quit. In fact, this was her pattern. Instead of speaking up for herself, she escaped uncomfortable work environments by quitting and moving to another company. This was exhausting and included moving her child to a new school. The problem was that Abby didn't change her behavior and she soon created the same challenges in her new workplace.

It was vital that Abby connect with her inner Diva to reclaim her power. I led her through my guided imagery process to meet this part of herself. During the session, her Diva gave Abby the unusual suggestion to always wear red shoes. She said red shoes are a subliminal power statement and it would help her stand her ground and speak her truth—like Dorothy's special ruby red slippers in The Wizard of Oz.

Abby was willing to try anything! She wore red shoes and even made red her signature color. Wearing red reminded Abby that her Diva was right there with her. Day-by-day, she worked diligently to improve her communication skills. She began to stand her ground and challenged people when it was necessary to keep her boundaries. Abby discovered that as soon as she believed in herself, other people did too.

In her effort to avoid conflict or disagreements, the Peacekeeper struggles to create the relationships she wants. This is frustrating, because she tries so hard to be thoughtful of others. Her strategy to stuff her feelings doesn't work. Often, a simple conversation could clear up misunderstandings, but she doesn't do this. Speaking up is the hardest thing for the Peacekeeper to do, but it is the one thing that will change her life.

Speaking up is the hardest thing for the Peacekeeper to do, but it is the one thing that will change her life.

— Wallflower Wanda —

If the Peacekeeper doesn't get a wake-up call, she crawls into her shell even further and gives up on herself and others! She becomes Wallflower Wanda who blends in and disappears. She doesn't believe anyone listens to her, so she doesn't see the point of sharing her opinions. She is convinced that her needs don't matter, so she stops communicating. This is how she deals with life—by not dealing with it. She isolates herself and hopes her problems will disappear.

As Wallflower Wanda bottles up her feelings, she becomes angry and resentful. The only way she knows how to express herself is by being passive-aggressive. A subtle dig here, a random jab there won't make her look bad, will it? The silent treatment is also one of her old favorites. The result is that her relationships are filled with miscommunication, misunderstanding and manipulation.

Because she doesn't communicate directly, her emotions go underground too. What we repress will be expressed, one way or another. Wallflower Wanda may find an outlet for her feelings through overeating, excessive shopping or other self-sabotaging behaviors. But once she learns to express herself fully, these behaviors are often no longer a big draw for her. Never underestimate the power of being fully expressed, heard and understood.

> ## Never underestimate the power of being fully expressed, heard and understood.

This book can help you recognize and avoid getting sucked into an unhealthy and even abusive relationship—one where you don't have a voice and your needs don't matter. However, if you are already in a relationship where speaking your truth could put you in a dangerous situation, it is important that you reach out to get help. Your safety is the priority.

Diva Up! Secrets
For The Peacekeeper

Take One New Step

There is tremendous wisdom that comes from taking one new step in the direction you want to go. One new step is as powerful as a giant leap, because you are moving in a new direction. When you face your fears, you create a new normal. Soon, you are dancing in Dorothy's ruby red slippers unwilling to let anything stand in the way of your power and your potential.

"This Is What Is True For Me"

You need to have a voice in all your relationships—a big voice. When you speak up, you may not always get a respectful dialogue in return. This can be uncomfortable. There is no guarantee someone will respond to you courteously. They may argue, get defensive, shame you or act disappointed. When faced with this pressure, hold your ground and simply say, "This is what is true for me." It is not your job to take care of the feelings of others. Your job is to tell the truth, your truth.

Express yourself and let the chips fall where they may. Trust that you can deal with whatever happens. Once you experience the immense power rush of speaking up and standing by your words, you will welcome every chance you have to do this.

Express yourself and let the chips
fall where they may. Trust that
you can deal with whatever happens.

Express Yourself

The Peacekeeper wants to maintain harmony, so she focuses on the feelings, thoughts and needs of others while ignoring her own. She prides herself in being the happy one, the calm one and the peaceful one. In this way, her real emotions can become backlogged. It isn't fair or healthy to block the flow of our feelings and emotions. It is vital to know and understand what we feel, so we can process and express those feelings.

Check in with yourself often to see how you really feel. You may be encountering challenging emotions such as anger, grief or depression. Welcome these emotions as part of your life's journey. When you let them flow, you let them go. Ignoring your feelings is not the solution. Holding on to negative emotions is unhealthy. When you honor your feelings, you honor yourself.

When you honor your feelings,
you honor yourself.

The Empowered Peacekeeper

When the Peacekeeper learns to DIVA UP, she no longer bottles up her emotions, stuffs her feelings or silences her voice. She takes a stand for what is true for her and fiercely creates boundaries. She knows they are not optional. As she gains the communication skills she needs, she takes control of her destiny.

Kindness matters, but so does honesty. Her self-mastery comes when she integrates her kindness with her strength to make her voice heard. She is not afraid to stand up for herself and she supports other women to do the same. She has gone from being a wallflower to a fierce lioness who is ready to roar. Her Diva superpowers are courage and honesty.

Her Diva superpowers are courage and honesty.

The Peacekeeper's Profile

Virtue: *Harmony*

Hidden Belief: *I am worthy if I am nice*

Disempowered Name: *Wallflower Wanda*

Challenge: *I don't speak up to express my needs, feelings, opinions and boundaries*

Emotion: *Passive-aggressive*

Solution: *Tell the truth. Express your point of view. Create and maintain boundaries*

Good Girl Healing: *I am still a kind person if I speak my truth. My voice matters*

Diva Superpowers: *Courage and honesty. (I am courageous and honest)*

The Peacekeeper's Prescription

✓ Create and keep boundaries

✓ Express yourself clearly

✓ Surround yourself with people who respect you

✓ Develop and use your communication skills

✓ Realize that you matter and your point of view is important

✓ Face your fears

✓ Be truthful

The person I need to
tell the truth to is...

The Pleaser

Virtue: *Love*

Hidden Belief: *I am worthy if I please others*

The Pleaser is a lovebug. She just wants to love and be loved. She is always smiling because she sees the world sunny-side up. Her wide-eyed innocence makes her *The Sweetheart* who is universally adored. You can recognize her energy because of the non-judgmental space she holds for you. She accepts you as you are, and this is her great gift. When you are around her, you are free to be yourself. She is a patient listener and loyal friend. The Pleaser represents the virtue of love. She is what you might imagine as the classic accommodating Good Girl. She is endearing but struggles to keep her boundaries or say, "No." She never wants to hurt anyone's feelings, even if it means abandoning herself. So, while the Peacekeeper doesn't fully speak up, the Pleaser doesn't fully show up.

The Pleaser hides her true self to get love and acceptance from others. When we stop being the queen of our own self-worth, we give our power away and abdicate our throne. Unfortunately, the more we do this, the less confident we feel. Eventually, we no longer feel we are worthy of what we want, nor powerful enough to create it.

> When we stop being the queen of
> our own self-worth, we give our power
> away and abdicate our throne.

The Pleaser is a chameleon who is adept at changing herself to accommodate the needs of others. She makes herself clay for others to mold. While it is healthy to make compromises in relationships, it is not healthy to abandon ourselves.

Jenn was a teenager who discovered she loved make-up. She had her own unique style which was an important part of her self-expression. But her mother didn't like Jenn to be self-expressive or to attract attention. She made negative comments every time Jenn wore make-up.

In the morning before school, they would have huge fights which resulted in Jenn washing her face. Every day, she would end up wearing less and less make-up hoping she could get out the door, but it never worked. Overtime, she just stopped wearing any make-up to avoid her mother's judgment. In doing so, she abandoned herself.

Her mother was afraid of Jenn's individuality and freedom. She felt threatened. She was a single mother who counted on her daughter for emotional support. Her daughter's independence made her feel insecure. Jenn learned to abandon herself to please and appease her mother.

She went through high school with the nickname "plain Jane," although she knew she had this incredible sense of style. She wore baggy clothes and never wore make-up because it was easier than fighting with her mother.

Jenn learned to bend to the will of others and accommodate their needs. It wasn't until she was in her thirties that she finally started on a path that was all her own. She went to cosmetology school, got her license and went into business as a make-up artist. She moved to Los Angeles and began doing make-up artistry in films. The good news is that the desire to be our true self never goes away, no matter how far afield we go.

The patient Pleaser has attended to the needs of others for so long, she is unsure about who she is and what she wants. She is indecisive. She puts all her energy into supporting the projects, goals and dreams of others. Meanwhile, she has a closet full of her own half-hoped-for dreams that have never seen the light of day. Everyone else comes first. To stop this self-abandonment spiral, the Pleaser needs to claim her own goals and ferociously protect how she spends her time. Of course, this must include learning how to say "No."

When we know our Good Girl Type, we have the insight and the wisdom to read the signs, signals and symptoms that tell us that we are playing small and giving our power away. One sign that you are caught in the Pleaser's trap is chronic under-earning.

Christine was a relationship coach and radio host who couldn't raise her prices. She had twenty years of professional experience, but her prices didn't reflect her expertise. Her Good Girl Type was the Pleaser/Fixer. Although she worked for herself, she gave me a long list of reasons why she couldn't charge more for her services.

- *She wanted to be liked.*

- *She didn't want to be pushy.*

- *She didn't want to be rejected.*

- *She wanted to be generous.*

- *She was sure that her clients would not pay more.*

Christine's prices were low for her industry and experience. I suggested she double her prices immediately for all her new incoming clients. This way she could avoid talking with her current clients about money. But Christine was resistant to my idea citing all the reasons above.

We talked about how she was abandoning herself and her life by not raising her prices. She even confessed to giving frequent discounts to her already low prices. Basically, Christine had turned her business into a thrift store— everything was a give-away.

Christine told me she felt powerful by just helping people. She said she received many intrinsic rewards beyond the remuneration she received. This was an important insight. If her work was meaningful and fulfilling, she let the money slide. But her business was not a charity—she needed to earn a living.

Money highlights our issues with our worth and power. Christine's security depended on her seeing money as an integral and valuable exchange for her helping services. Understanding her struggle, I invited Christine to connect with her inner Diva. In our guided imagery session, her Diva suggested that she adopt a new motto:

"I set my prices to be respected, not liked."

Christine said she liked being respected, so she agreed she would try this with her next new client. To her surprise, her client didn't flinch when she quoted her new higher price. She couldn't believe it was so easy to set this precedent. Christine felt excited and agreed to double her prices for all incoming clients. She couldn't afford to go back to giving her services away.

For the first time in years, she felt hopeful that she could continue to do the work she loved so much—helping people. It seemed like the more money she requested, the more her clients were interested in working with her. Her new higher prices let her clients know that her work was of great value, she was highly skilled and she knew her worth.

This whole process catapulted Christine into the awareness that she wanted to take a stand for her value. She had been absolutely convinced that she needed to keep her prices low and herself small, but not anymore!

This scenario often happens to women in the helping professions—they can't reconcile earning money with helping people. Christine couldn't see that she had been devaluing herself. Years of living by the Good Girl mantra, "I don't matter," had become her way of life.

The Pleaser separates herself from her earning power because she believes it is virtuous to shrink her needs. She literally pushes money away and falls into financial disempowerment. The Pleaser has a poverty consciousness and thus assumes that everyone else has a poverty consciousness too. This is why it is so hard for her to make money, ask for the raise or charge what she is worth. By understanding her Good Girl psychology, Christine was able to make profound changes in her business and life. Her new motto became "I'm worth it."

Her new motto became "I'm worth it."

— Doormat Dottie —

If the Pleaser doesn't get a wake-up call, she lets people walk all over her. Doormat Dottie only wants to see the best in people. To do this, she ignores her intuition and overlooks the obvious truth. This doesn't turn out well for her. When she buries her head in the sand, her innocence turns to ignorance.

Doormat Dottie can attract space-invaders and manipulators and let them take over the reins of her life. She goes along with the program in order to make them happy, and to be accepted. At her worst, she lets them dictate her actions and even orchestrate her emotions. The Pleaser can end up feeling like a victim of the people to whom she has handed over her power.

Being a kind and empathic woman is wonderful, but don't just assume that people are who they say they are. Pay attention to their actions. If they don't match up to their words, face the truth. Being kind-hearted comes with a responsibility—to do what is best for yourself.

Being kind-hearted comes
with a responsibility—
to do what is best for yourself.

Diva Up! Secrets
For The Pleaser

I love myself enough to tell you "No."

When people request your time, energy or money, you have the right to say "No" to them. But once you do, they may not like it. They may keep pushing you because they want to get their way. All they have to do is push you enough, guilt you enough, and pressure you enough and you might give in. You cave because you think it means you are a good and kind person. Don't fall for this! Pleasing others at your own expense does not mean you are a good person. It means you don't value yourself enough to keep your boundaries.

> Pleasing others at your own expense
> does not mean you are a good person.
> It means you don't value yourself
> enough to keep your boundaries.

Be on high alert if someone tries to guilt-trip you or shame you when you say "No" to them. You have a right to decide what works for you at all times. You do not have to defend, explain or apologize for saying "No." Protect your energy from the demands of others. When you learn to say "No," you take back control of your life.

Be True to You

As a Pleaser, you may be letting people tell you who you *should* be. If someone insists that you give up your authentic self-expression, run the other way. Cultivate friends who genuinely celebrate you and encourage you to be yourself. Friends with an agenda aren't your friends. You are who you are for a unique purpose. There is no reason to change yourself in any way. Always be true to you.

> Cultivate friends who genuinely
> celebrate you and encourage you
> to be exactly who you are.

Take a "Diva-cation"

It is important that you take time away just for yourself. Give yourself space to discover who you are and what you desire. Create a Diva-cation retreat where you can clear your mind of everyone's needs and focus on your own. From this place, you can connect with your true feelings and true self. Plan your new empowered future—one where you are in charge of your destiny and you play the starring role!

> Give yourself permission to discover who
> you are and what you want.

The Empowered Pleaser

When the Pleaser learns to DIVA UP, she is no longer a pushover or a doormat. She holds her boundaries, listens to her intuition and takes full control of her destiny. She is not afraid of owning her worth and power. She takes center stage as the star of her own life.

The Empowered Pleaser does not abdicate her throne. She doesn't allow people into her world who don't respect her. No one can fool her or *use* her anymore. Her eyes are wide-open.

As the Pleaser protects her energy from the needs and agendas of others, she is finally able to live up to her potential by fulfilling her own goals and dreams. In doing so, she becomes a powerful creatrix who takes charge of her own success and happiness. Her Diva Superpowers are worthiness and strength.

Her Diva Superpowers are worthiness and strength.

The Pleaser's Profile

Virtue: *Love*

Hidden Belief: *I am worthy if I accommodate others (please people)*

Disempowered Name: *Doormat Dottie*

Challenge: *I abandon myself to please others*

Emotion: *Indecision. Self-doubt*

Solution: *Become the leading lady of your life. Take charge of your destiny*

Good Girl Healing: *I am still a good person if I say "No." I matter*

Diva Superpowers: *Worthiness and strength. (I am worthy. I am strong)*

The Pleaser's Prescription

- ✓ Realize that not everyone is going to like you, no matter how nice you are

- ✓ Master the art of saying "No"

- ✓ Listen to and trust your intuition

- ✓ Get in touch with your own feelings and needs

- ✓ Take charge of your destiny. Play the starring role

- ✓ Accept your worth and power

- ✓ Activate your goals and dreams

Am I changing my essential
self to meet the needs
of someone else?

The Fixer

Virtue: *Compassion*

Hidden Belief: *I am worthy if I am generous*

The Fixer is the classic do-gooder gal. She oozes generosity. You know her by her magnetic presence. She is like Mrs. Claus—ready to feed you cookies and assist with whatever your heart desires. People are attracted to her healing presence and she is attracted to helping them. She represents the virtue of compassion. She can't stand to see anyone or anything suffer. At her best, she is a beacon of hope in the lives of others.

Being generous is her idea of power. But while the Fixer is superwoman for others, she often doesn't bestow her own superpowers upon herself. She resists receiving. She likes to be a giver, and not a taker. With generosity as the core of her personality, she has a special knack for creating imbalances in her relationships. She can accidently take over the responsibilities of others. Often, the Fixer needs to back off from solving other people's problems in order to find her balance again.

Kiara had no problem marrying a man with four young children and taking on the role of step mom. At first she was excited about her new life. She was a nurturer—she loved being there for people. She was thirty six years old and felt desperate to have her own family. She hoped to get pregnant as soon as possible.

She quit her well-paying job as a financial advisor to step into this new role. Soon though, her husband was spending less and less time with the family, leaving all the work to Kiara. He had been very thoughtful and attentive during their courtship, but now that behavior disappeared with the realities of everyday life. He somehow managed to always be busy at work. Kiara had extraordinary nurturing skills and her husband did not, so he thought it was best to leave those duties to her.

Kiara hoped she would have an equal partner in raising their four children. But the more she made requests of him, the more he resisted. Kiara couldn't speak up without her husband getting upset and storming out of the room. She felt alone in her marriage. This wasn't the experience she had signed up for.

Taking on the roles of step mom and wife sounded great when her husband was present and involved, but now she felt alone in all the household duties. It was a real dilemma for her because there were children involved.

When Kiara took the Good Girl Questionnaire, she scored off the charts as a Fixer. Knowing her Good Girl Type helped her see exactly how she had created this situation.

I helped Kiara make a connection with her truth-telling Diva who showed Kiara what her life could look like if she were balanced in her giving and receiving. This included Kiara backing off her household duties in order to balance the scales. This would allow her husband a chance to step up to the plate. Kiara realized she was over-doing and not leaving any room for her husband to participate.

Kiara knew that she couldn't shoulder all the work, but now she knew what to do about it. With her new clarity, she sat down with her husband to talk about the situation. She told him they needed to work together as full partners. Her husband admitted that he was overwhelmed too, but wanted to help. They agreed to seek professional help in learning how to communicate with each other. They also realized they needed help, so they hired a part-time nanny. The entire burden of the household was no longer on Kiara's shoulders.

Once Kiara established boundaries, things began to shift. Recognizing herself as a Fixer, she knew she needed to make changes within herself first. If she didn't, she would have suffered in silence or packed her bags and left. There is a difference between service and sacrifice. The Fixer is empowered when she understands this difference. Giving ourselves up, and giving ourselves away, is never empowering.

> There is a difference between service and sacrifice. The Fixer is empowered when she understands this difference.

The Fixer tends to over-do for others. She wants everyone to be happy and she feels responsible for their happiness. Whatever she can do to tend to the well-being of others, she is there. The challenge for the Fixer is in setting boundaries with her generosity.

— Fix-It Fran —

If the Fixer doesn't get a wake-up call, she becomes the resident codependent and enabler Fix-It Fran. She rushes in to help people, which is admirable, but she can end up doing all their work for them and abandoning herself badly in the process. As well, the other person doesn't get a chance to discover their strength by solving their own challenges.

Fix-It Fran won't leave someone who needs her, even if she knows they are *using* her. She will sacrifice everything she has before she abandons someone who (she perceives) needs her help. Leaving a relationship with a needy person is not easy for anyone, but it is Fix-It Fran's worst nightmare.

Fifty year old Bianca was in a relationship with Art, a man twenty years younger. Art had a multitude of problems that Bianca was more than happy to take on. She was eternally optimistic that all the love, devotion and money she invested in Art would eventually pay off. She believed he could straighten himself out with all her generous care, and she was in love. Bianca assumed Art would mature, so he could be what she needed him to be—a full life partner. All the while, Bianca's life was zipping past her.

Art's challenges were way too big for Bianca to solve, but she didn't want to give up on him—on love. His life was an endless stream of trauma drama, which he brought upon himself. Bianca was always there by his side, no matter what the problem.

Ten years passed and Bianca turned sixty years old. Bianca had changed and grown, but Art was the same person he'd always been. He was still floundering through life. Problems stuck to him like Velcro, and Bianca felt responsible for bailing him out every time. The more needy Art became, the more Bianca rescued him. Over the years he even borrowed large sums of money from her and never repaid it.

Bianca became like a mother to Art—one who would never consider abandoning her child regardless of the cost to her. If she broke up with him, she would be abandoning a needy person and that would make her a bad person. This is the Fixer's trap.

Finally, Art found someone his own age who wasn't always trying to change him and he left Bianca. When he broke up with her, he never expressed his appreciation for all the love and support she offered him. He just wasn't capable of expressing his appreciation, and never had been.

Fix-It Fran has a tendency to attract relationships where she ends up trying to fix the other person. She holds out hope, against all odds, that the other person will change. In the process, she can let her life force (and even her bank account) get strained and drained to the breaking point. Being generous is great, but betraying ourselves is not.

It isn't wise to enter into relationships with the hope that the other person will change. It sets up a bad dynamic and is a recipe for disappointment and even disaster from the start.

Being generous is great, but betraying ourselves is not.

Diva Up! Secrets
For The Fixer

Create A "Diva Day!"

Self-care is about celebrating your needs instead of denying them. Take off your superwoman cape and let people express their affection for you. Just as you enjoy appreciating people with your generosity, give those around you the chance to do the same for you!

Create a "Diva Day" for yourself. Put on a tiara, or perhaps a purple boa. Create a Diva-Do list, so people know what you want them from them. This is your chance to receive from others, and even to be pampered! It is healthy to keep the scales balanced between giving and receiving. The benefits will reverberate throughout your life.

Self-care is about celebrating your needs instead of denying them.

Hold on to Your Wallet

Money is another way you try to love and care for people. You think nothing of opening your wallet for those in need, but make sure you don't put your own needs aside in your eagerness to help. Your indomitable spirit to solve, heal, help and fix the problems of others can leave you empty-handed and without options, if you aren't paying attention. It's important to keep your financial boundaries. I wish I had known I was a Fixer in my twenties. I wouldn't have sold the stock my father had given me. I mindlessly used it to help a boyfriend solve his problems. If I had held onto it, that stock would have been worth a great deal today. If I had known I was a Fixer, I would have said, "No" to solving his problems at my expense. As a full-fledged, out-of-control Fixer, I thought nothing of selling my stock, giving away the proceeds, and asking for nothing in return. It has taken me many years to know that I am still a good person if I consider my own needs.

You are still a good person if you consider your own needs.

"Not My Business"

You want to help everyone, but the truth is you can't. And, there are times when you shouldn't. "NMB" (not my business) is a phrase you can use when you really need to consider whether taking on a certain project is right for you. Don't worry! There is no chance you will stop being compassionate, but you will choose carefully who and how you help.

"NMB" let's you push the pause button, so you can decide if this is your project to take on. Often the Good Girl feels ashamed for thinking of her own needs. When you DIVA UP, you don't apologize for doing what is right for you.

The Empowered Fixer

The Fixer's self-mastery comes when she learns to balance the scales between giving and receiving. She no longer rejects support that is offered. She includes herself in her equation of compassion.

The Empowered Fixer has learned how to be of service without sacrificing herself. She employs a temperance in her generosity. She can say "No" when it is necessary. The Empowered Fixer can pull back her energy in order to give others a chance to contribute. In doing so, she becomes the wise priestess who governs her life from a place of true strength and compassion. Her Diva Superpowers are creating boundaries and receiving.

Her Diva Superpowers are creating boundaries & receiving.

The Fixer's Profile

Virtue: *Compassion*

Hidden Belief: *I am worthy if I am generous*

Disempowered Name: *Fix-it Fran*

Challenge: *I over-give and over-do for others*

Emotion: *Resentment*

Solution: *Develop temperance with your generosity. Create and maintain boundaries*

Good Girl Healing: *I am still a generous person if I consider my own needs. My needs matter*

Diva Superpowers: *Creating boundaries and receiving. Create and maintain your boundaries*

The Fixer's Prescription

✓   Make your boundaries clear

✓   Allow others to give to you—receive

✓   Let people know what you need from them

✓   Don't do other people's work for them

✓   Make sure you are not betraying yourself when you help someone else

✓   Love yourself as much as you love others

Am I over-giving in
some area of my life?
What needs to change?

The Perfectionist

Virtue: *Purity*

Hidden Belief: *I am worthy if I am perfect*

The Perfectionist Good Girl is the *can-do* woman. Reliable, dutiful and hardworking, she earns her accomplishments. She isn't expecting anything to be handed to her. With her strong work ethic and high standards, prepare to be blown away by what she achieves. She represents the virtue of purity and this means that living up to her potential is not optional for her. She is on it every minute of every day. She is a talented visionary who is always seeking to improve herself and the world. At her best, she is a changemaker.

It may be hard to recognize the Perfectionist as a Good Girl. She appears ultra-competent and confident, but she is in her own Good Girl trap. The Perfectionist decides that if she if perfect, she is worthy. But even more, she believes that by being perfect, she is *good*. She derives her sense of value from the following formula:

I am worthy *and good* if I am perfect

The Perfectionist does not accept anything less than perfection from herself. What this really means is that she does not accept *herself*. You can imagine this puts a great deal of pressure on her. She has to prove her worth in everything she does. In this way, she becomes her own taskmaster.

The Perfectionist loves to expand, improve and be on the move. She is driven to achieve. She cracks the whip to get her gold star or to grab the brass ring. She believes that being mediocre tells the world you are lazy, and that doesn't garner respect or admiration. The more accomplishments, titles, accolades, acknowledgments, awards, degrees and success she acquires, the better she feels about herself.

The problem is, the Perfectionist doesn't always feel worthy or deserving of her accomplishments. She never feels *good enough*. With her discriminating eye, she spends endless amounts of time and energy looking at her flaws. She wants to shave down those pounds. She agonizes over balancing her checkbook. She prides herself on never being late and on being the perfect Good Girl. Her passion to be her *best* puts her on a hamster wheel where she works hard, but never feels that she is *good enough*.

The Perfectionist will work her fingers to the bone to make sure everyone is happy and everything is perfect. She is no stranger to putting on a big show to appear perfect. Appearances are everything to her. Showing up half-ass is the Perfectionists worst nightmare.

> ## She is no stranger to putting on a big show to appear perfect. Appearances are everything to her.

The Perfectionist Good Girl can be fiercely competitive. She can make her life a contest to win the attention, admiration and validation of others. She imagines that if she were just good enough, she would finally receive the love and acceptance from others that she craves. In order to do this, she beleives she needs to win out over other people, as if there is only so much love to go around. We learn our patterns as children. The Perfectionist learned that she could garner love, attention and admiration if she excelled. There is nothing wrong with striving to be your best or in taking pride in your accomplishments, but there is a line. Striving to make yourself better (perfect) can disconnect you from your true self. You can end up having everything you want but not being happy or fulfilled. In your zeal to accomplish one more thing, make sure you don't forget what is truly important.

Sophie was an exhausted Perfectionist whose to-do list kept expanding. She regularly worked hours past midnight because she couldn't say "No" to people who made requests of her.

She believed the harder she worked the more important she was. This meant she piled responsibilities on herself. To her, being busy meant she was valuable. The problem was that this stole her life force. Clients called her on the spur of the moment and asked favors of her, and she eagerly agreed to support them. This often meant hours of unpaid work for Sophie.

Her days were jam-packed full. There was not a minute to spare, and yet she wasn't enjoying her life. In our coaching sessions, she didn't understand the concept of taking some downtime for herself. She wasn't even making time to enjoy being with her husband and son. Every day was rush, rush, rush. Accomplishment was very important to her, so she hustled all day long, afraid of making mistakes or of being late.

The truth was that she really didn't need to hustle or make extra work for herself. She could make her own schedule. Even so, she worked herself to the bone and was unhappy.

Her relationships with her son and husband were strained to the breaking point. She put a lot of pressure on them to be perfect as well. She hated making mistakes, so she couldn't accept blunders from them either.

I helped Sophie meet her inner Diva who showed her the reason she was creating an overloaded schedule—to prove her worth. After connecting with her Diva, she felt empowered to make sweeping changes. She no longer conducted her life from unworthiness with the need to prove her value. This meant saying "No" to spur of the moment requests. She limited her evening events to twice a week. This helped her find room in *her schedule for new activities. She chose enjoyable activities that were not focused on achievement.*

At first, it was hard for Sophie to get used to having some downtime in her day. She had never done this before, but soon she was enjoying her freedom. She did some decorating, some baking and made time to be with her husband and son— including going on a long vacation together. She also made time to connect with herself by beginning a practice of yoga and meditation.

Sophie realized that she loved taking control of her schedule. She liked being the boss of her life. Her schedule no longer controlled her. She was in charge and she liked that! It was up to her to create the life that she really wanted. She just needed to slow down to discover what was truly important to her.

— Polly Perfect Pants —

If the Perfectionist doesn't get a wake-up call, she becomes Polly Perfect Pants where she pushes herself and others to meet her own uncompromising standards. No one can accommodate all her demands, but that doesn't stop her from trying. She needs everyone around her to be perfect too. Since she works hard, she is judgmental of people who don't have her same work ethic.

Polly Perfect Pants takes the Good Girl Rules very seriously. She is, of course, the perfect Good Girl. She takes special pride in knowing the *right* way to be a good person. If someone doesn't conform to her ideas of the *right* way to be, she judges them. She can end up driving people away. No one wants to be under her microscopic eye where their every move is analyzed and judged.

Diva Up! Secrets
For The Perfectionist

Take Imperfect Action

Sometimes the Perfectionist is not an overachiever. Instead, she is immobilized. She is afraid of taking imperfect action, because she fears being seen as inadequate. For the immobilized Perfectionist, anything less than perfection is failure. She is terrified of the judgment of others and of her own judgment, so she doesn't move forward. If she tries and fails, it would be unbearable. If she tries and falls short, she would feel humiliated. She can't handle it, so she sits on the sidelines and spins her wheels.

The Immobilized Perfectionist is not inadequate, she just fears that she is. The remedy for the Immobilized Perfectionist is to take imperfect action. As soon as she gets her projects off the ground, she learns that imperfection isn't the worst thing that could happen—sitting on the sidelines is!

Imperfection isn't the worst thing that could happen—sitting on the sidelines is!

Bring Your Real Self To The Party Of Life

Pay attention to the ways in which you don't express your true self in order to maintain a perfect image to others. Everyone around you is used to your perfect image. You know how to handle every situation. You don't want to bother anyone by showing up as a real person.

Hiding your real self doesn't allow you to live fully—it's the Perfectionist's trap. It is impossible to be happy or healthy if you don't express your full spectrum of emotions and feelings.

Recognize the ways in which you wear a mask to appear perfect. What are you hiding? What is the cost of doing this? What are you losing out on in this process? The secret to reclaiming your power as a Perfectionist is to bring your real self to the party of life.

> Recognize the ways in which you
> wear a mask to appear perfect.
> What is the cost of doing this?

Toss Out Your "To-Do" List

You want to accomplish as much as is humanly possible, so you load up your schedule and forge ahead with your nose to the grindstone. Sometimes, the answer is not to *be* more or to *do* more. For the striving Perfectionist, it is often unstructured downtime that is the most beneficial.

Make a date to enjoy being in nature or schedule relaxed time with friends and family. Toss out your to-do list and go with the flow. When you practice *being* instead of *doing*, you reap the rewards of replenishing on a deep soul level. This brings a fresh clarity and insight into everything you do, and it helps you pursue things that are truly of value to you.

> When you practice *being* instead of
> *doing*, you reap the rewards of
> replenishing on a deep soul level.

The Empowered Perfectionist

When the Perfectionist learns to DIVA UP, she no longer lives for the validation of others. She has sorted out the lies she tells herself about what makes her worthy and good. The first thing she does is loosen up on the demands she makes of herself, and others. Second, she realizes that her need to be *right* puts everyone on edge. Third, she pumps the brakes on her need to achieve, so she can experience what is of true value to her. Finally, she takes off her mask of perfection and lets herself be a real person...flaws and all!

The Empowered Perfectionist knows her worth doesn't come from being perfect, or by putting on a front to impress others. There is no such thing as perfection. She is already perfectly imperfect, and so is everyone else. Now, she jumps into life with both feet.

When the Perfectionist learns to DIVA UP, she becomes a messenger for others to accept themselves as they are. Her Diva superpowers are self-acceptance and understanding. She accepts herself as she is and others as they are.

Her Diva superpowers are self-acceptance and understanding

The Perfectionist's Profile

Virtue: *Purity*

Hidden Belief: *I am worthy if I am perfect and beyond judgment*

Disempowered Name: *Polly Perfect Pants*

Challenge: *I over-achieve to prove my worth*

Emotion: *Judgment*

Solution: *Let go of needing to be perfect*

Good Girl Healing: *I am still a worthy person if I am my true self. My true self matters*

Diva Superpower: *Self-acceptance and understanding. (I accept myself as I am and others as they are.)*

The Perfectionist's Prescription

✓   Focus on what is truly meaningful to you

✓   Process and express your real emotions

✓   Give up the idea that you have to be perfect

✓   Accept who you are. Accept others as they are

✓   Let go of the need for approval from others

✓   Relax your need to be *right*

✓   Plan for downtime without an agenda

What do I need to let
go of to make room for
what is meaningful to me?

Summary of the Good Girl Types

The Good Girl thinks she is a bad person if she considers her own needs. This is precisely how she gives her power away. When you crack your Good Girl code, you don't play this game of self-betrayal and self-abandonment. You simply acknowledge what is right for you and stand by it.

The 4 Good Girl Types show us precisely how we can create disempowering patterns in our life.

- *Perhaps you stuff your feelings to avoid conflict like the Peacekeeper.*

- *Or, maybe you let other people define you like the Pleaser.*

- *You could over-give in your relationships like the Fixer.*

- *Or, you might be a Perfectionist who drives herself into the ground to prove her worth.*

Sometimes we have to lose our self in order to find our way again. As you have seen, each Good Girl Type is empowered to the extent that she makes herself a priority—when she values herself as much as she values others. Each Good Girl Type has her own healing.

> Each Good Girl is empowered to the
> extent that she makes herself a priority.

GOOD GIRL Healing Statements

The Peacekeeper

I am still a kind person if I speak my truth.
My voice matters.

The Pleaser

I am still a good person if I say, "No."
I matter.

The Fixer

I am still a generous person if I consider my own needs.
My needs matter.

The Perfectionist

I am still a worthy person if I am my true self.
My true self matters.

One of the best parts of life is caring for others. The Good Girl is well aware of this. She knows what a privilege it is to help others. Whether it is taking care of her own children, her elderly parents, a disabled sibling or an ill friend or partner, sometimes we are called to give selflessly—to be the stewards of others. It is an honor to usher people through their life passages and to be a part of it.

The Good Girl still needs to find her balance in these situations. She needs to put herself in the picture, so she can keep her boundaries. With your Diva by your side, you are not abandoning others—you are including yourself.

When you DIVA UP you are not abandoning others—you are including yourself.

When we keep our boundaries, we can fully give to others without expectations. We have taken care of ourselves, so there will be no resentment or unfulfilled expectations waiting for us on the other side. This is a great gift we give ourselves and others.

Take time to process what you have learned about your Good Girl Type. It's your life. You are the leading lady as well as the director, producer and script writer! With your Diva by your side, you step into your leading lady role and take center stage. You are not playing a bit part and you are not an understudy to anyone else.

Creating a life you love is a commitment you make to yourself. You now have the wisdom, and the tools, to make profound changes. Plan on taking new actions, so you can benefit from getting new results. Start now!

Summary Charts of the Good Girl Types

— The Peacekeeper's Profile —

Virtue: *Harmony*

Hidden Belief: *I am worthy if I am nice*

Disempowered Name: *Wallflower Wanda*

Challenge: *I don't speak up to express my needs, feelings, opinions and boundaries*

Emotion: *Passive-aggressive*

Solution: *Tell the truth. Express your point of view. Create and maintain boundaries*

Good Girl Healing: *I am still a kind person when I speak my truth. My voice matters*

Diva Superpowers: *Courage and honesty. (I am courageous and honest)*

— The Pleaser's Profile —

Virtue: *Love*

Hidden Belief: *I am worthy if I accommodate others (please people)*

Disempowered Name: *Doormat Dottie*

Challenge: *I abandon myself to please others*

Emotion: *Indecision. Self-doubt*

Solution: *Become the leading lady of your life. Take charge of your destiny*

Good Girl Healing: *I am still a good person if I say, "No." I matter*

Diva Superpowers: *Worthiness and strength. (I am worthy. I am strong)*

— The Fixer's Profile —

Virtue: *Compassion*

Hidden Belief: *I am worthy if I am generous*

Disempowered Name: *Fix-it Fran*

Challenge: *I over-give and over-do for others*

Emotion: *Resentment*

Solution: *Develop temperance with your generosity. Create and maintain your boundaries*

Good Girl Healing: *I am still a generous person if I consider my own needs. My needs matter*

Diva Superpowers: *Creating boundaries and receiving. (I create boundaries and accept help)*

— The Perfectionist's Profile —

Virtue: *Purity*

Hidden Belief: *I am worthy if I am perfect and beyond judgment*

Disempowered Name: *Polly Perfect Pants*

Challenge: *I over-achieve to prove my worth*

Emotion: *Judgment*

Solution: *Let go of needing to be perfect and right*

Good Girl Healing: *I am still a worthy person if I am my true self. My real self matters*

Diva Superpower: *Self-acceptance and understanding. (I accept myself as I am and others as they are)*

On the next page you will put everything you have learned together to create your Good Girl Blueprint.

The Good Girl Blueprint

My Good Girl Type is:

The Peacekeeper / The Fixer

My Virtues are:

Harmony / Compassion

My Diva Superpowers are:

Courage & Honesty / Creating Boundaries & Receiving

My Disempowered Names are:

Wallflower Wanda / Fix-it Fran

My Good Girl Healing is:

My voice matters / My needs matter

My Power Mantra is: (from page 38)

"I Dream Bigger"

My Good Girl Blueprint

My Good Girl Type is:

_____ / _____

My Virtues are:

_____ / _____

My Diva Superpowers are:

_____ / _____

My Disempowered Names are:

_____ / _____

My Good Girl Healing is:

_____ / _____

My Power Mantra is: (from page 38)

_____

Your Sovereignty

14

Power Play #5
Heal Your Unappreciated Good Girl

My grievances hide the light of the world in me.
—Lesson 69, *A Course in Miracles*

Without our Diva's ability to tell the truth and keep boundaries, our Good Girl spins her wheels. Like a tire in a mud ditch, she repeats the same self-sabotaging patterns over and over. If nothing changes over the years, she can become an Unappreciated Good Girl. It is often difficult to recognize and acknowledge this part of ourselves, but we know what she sounds like:

People use me

I give and others take

People try to control me

People don't respect me

Money seems to elude me

I am not getting what I deserve

I work very hard, but I feel unfulfilled

People don't respect my boundaries

People take advantage of my generosity

People don't keep their agreements with me

Ah ... the joy of being an Unappreciated Good Girl! It may be painful to recognize some of these statements as your own, especially when all you do is give, give and then give some more! In fact, it's infuriating! You wonder why you always end up with the short end of the stick. You know you deserve so much better, and so much more for all your efforts. You're a good person after all!

Power Play #5
Heal your Unappreciated Good Girl

The Unappreciated Good Girl is convinced that she gives and others take. It all comes to a boiling point when she realizes she hasn't received her fair share of the pie in life. People aren't appreciating her for all she has done for them, and now she needs someone to blame for her stockpile of resentments and unfulfilled dreams.

The Unappreciated Good Girl feels like a victim, so everyone becomes a mirror upon which she projects her long standing resentments, anger and insecurities. The reliable, predictable Good Girl becomes explosive and unpredictable. She is at the end of her rope. But the Good Girl has played a big part in creating her own disappointments by:

- *Not speaking up, but expecting others to understand her needs and point of view.*

- *Not creating boundaries, but being angry when her boundaries are crossed.*

- *Over-giving, and then feeling betrayed when people don't do their fair share.*

- *Abandoning herself in the process of helping others.*

- *Repressing her worth and value.*

- *Having distorted ideas about what people owe her.*

We all deserve an abundant, love-filled life. We can create this for ourselves, but not if we have a chip on our shoulder. Holding on to grudges only weighs us down and limits our creative power. Our ego mind thrives on judging and on being *right*, so it loves justified anger. This means it is easy to get caught up in the victim/blame game.

The victim/blame game is a detour on our path to living powerfully, as anyone who has gone down this route can tell you. In fact, it's a dead end. The Good Girl can find herself on this path for years if she doesn't have the insight, support and tools to DIVA UP!

The victim/blame game is a detour on our path to power.

Your empowered future is waiting for you! Now is the time to listen to your intuition, keep your boundaries and make yourself a priority. You may feel justified directing negative energy toward people you perceive have betrayed you, but this won't help you create the life you really want. When you hold people hostage in your mind, you imprison yourself. Sometimes we need to take time out to heal our hurts and forgive people before we can move on. But the Unappreciated Good Girl can get stuck in a victim/blame cycle and let it control her. This means she doesn't move on.

Make a list of your grudges and grievances. Commit to letting them go. You don't need them. You have bigger and better things to do with your life. You are not here to be anyone's judge and jury. This doesn't mean you have to be around people you don't trust. It means you stop harboring anger and resentment towards them.

— Withholding Love —

The Unappreciated Good Girl can make herself a victim not only of others, but of herself. I was once on a retreat in Hawaii. Everything about it was truly magical. There was nothing to complain about—unless you needed to complain of course. I had a roommate—a woman

I had never met before. She was 6 feet tall and striking.

One day on the way to breakfast, I felt that she could use a compliment, so I told her she was stunning. As soon as the words came out of my mouth, I knew I had stepped on a land mine. Sound the alarm! She dove into her big victim excuse. What was it? She was too tall and it was ruining her life. I had pressed her special, secret misery button and she blew up! For the rest of the retreat, I heard a million ways you can suffer if you are tall. I opened the floodgates with a simple compliment.

We all have our own misery button and suffering story. It's the reason we use to feel like a victim of life. It's that special thought that circles and dive bombs us on a regular basis. It could be about your money, your body, your parents, your children, your relationship or something else.

What is your special, secret misery button (suffering story)?

I feel like a victim because:

I make myself a victim because:

The truth is, we have the power to love ourselves just as we are! To get there, we need grit and grace. At some point we learn that it isn't actually our perceived flaws that hold us back in life—it's our unwillingness to love ourselves.

Our flaws don't actually hold us back— it's our unwillingness to love ourselves.

We all have a choice to make. We can live as a victim or we can claim our worth and power. Life is full of challenges and struggles. No one is perfect and life is not perfect. We will experience disappointments. But when we don't recognize the part we play in creating and maintaining our own suffering stories, misery envelops us like a giant cloud of pink cotton candy. Everywhere we turn, it sticks to us. We are caught in a web of our own suffering. It is impossible to rule our queendom powerfully in this way, and it isn't fun either!

You are empowered when you take 100% responsibility for creating your own suffering stories. You decide how you react to life. Take time to process your feelings and disappointments. But plan to get back on your throne as soon as possible so you can rule your world as the powerful priestess that you are. When you are in touch with your inner Diva, you don't put your happiness on hold. You don't let your suffering stories overtake your joy. You are important now! Your life matters. You matter.

Whoever you have to forgive, do it and free yourself. Flick that victim chip off your shoulder and take your power back. Your love is your greatest power—use it wisely!

Don't let your suffering stories overtake your joy.

What suffering story am I
holding on to?

Who am I punishing?

15

Shine Your Light

As we let our light shine, we unconsciously give other people permission to do the same.

—Marianne Williamson

Perhaps you have experienced the soul crushing pain of living in disguise as a smaller version of yourself—of dimming yourself down. You know you are capable of so much more, but you hold yourself back.

Just like a seed bursting through the ground to become a flower, we all feel the urge to expand into our most radiant self. Each one of us has a mission to make a difference in the world in our own unique way. Sometimes this urge is loud and clear, and other times it is a distant, faint whisper. We respond to this inner call in many different ways. We can turn our face toward the sun to draw in its life-giving nourishment, but just as quickly turn away. We are afraid to shine. The good news is, this call to shine never goes away because it is the call to know and express our true self.

Power Play #6
Shine Your Light

The fear of shining our light is actually the fear of revealing our worth and power. As we have seen throughout this book, women can be power-deniers. Up until this point, we have looked at how we deny our own power, but we can also deny power in other women. If we want to live powerfully, we need to understand how we reject feminine power.

> If we want to live powerfully,
> we need to understand how we
> reject feminine power

— The Feminine Power Shadow —

Women who are power-deniers play a game called, *"I'll hide my power if you will hide yours."* In this game, everyone plays small so no one feels threatened. If anyone expands beyond the unspoken Good Girl boundaries, the power-deniers will let you know it! They throw the Good Girl Rule Book at you to herd you back into the corral. For example:

- *If you make money, they might say you don't care about people—you're selfish.*

- *If you create good fortune for yourself, they might say you slept your way to the top.*

- *If you gain recognition and notoriety, they might say that you don't deserve your good fortune—you were just lucky.*

- *If you experience success, they might spread gossip that you are dishonest or greedy.*

I call this phenomenon The Feminine Power Shadow. The simple truth is that if we don't accept our own power, we won't accept power in other women. The idea that women would try to diminish each other is beyond infuriating! It goes against everything that women stand for: collaboration, community, compassion and caring. It is important to understand that if we judge and criticize women who show up in their value, it backfires keeping us in our own Good Girl straightjacket.

If we don't accept our own power, we won't accept power in other women.

The Feminine Power Shadow can loom over us like a dark foreboding cloud. Instead of celebrating our success and expansion, we feel ashamed and afraid of our power. The Good Girl will shut down when faced with The Feminine Power Shadow, so we need to understand it.

Jessica was on the verge of substantial success and notoriety, but she held back and couldn't figure out why. Her fear was that she would make other women uncomfortable if she excelled. She told me:

- *She did not want to make anyone feel bad about themselves, as she experienced extraordinary success.*

- *She did not want to experience the judgment and jealousy of other women.*

- *She hated the thought of being judged as a self-centered or vain person.*

- *She wanted to be liked.*

- *She worried she would be abandoned by friends if she up-leveled her life.*

Jessica was at a standstill with her fears. She knew she could not control the judgements of others, so she tried to hold back the forward momentum of her own success. The result was that she was letting big opportunities pass her by.

When I explained to Jessica that she was experiencing the Feminine Power Shadow, all the puzzle pieces fell into place. Now she could face this energy and stand up to it. Previously, she was fighting an enemy she could not see or understand.

When you play a bigger game, you need your fierce and fearless Diva on your team. She knows it isn't your business to monitor the judgements of others. Not everyone will adore you when you up-level. It's time to put your big girl panties on and get over it!

> Not everyone will adore you when you up-level. It's time to put your big girl panties on and get over it!

— It's a Diva Emergency! —

There is nothing you can do about how other women react to your empowerment. Every woman must come to terms with her own power-outage. If someone needs to tear you down to feel good about themselves, they are having a Diva emergency! Their Diva is trying to emerge. The more aware you are of the Feminine Power Shadow, the less you will let it control you.

When you accept, respect, and celebrate your worth and power, it will ruffle someone's feathers. You can count on it. But never play small to make other women comfortable. Instead, invite other women to own their worth and power too. Ultimately, this is what women want the most—to know that they are worthy, powerful and unlimited.

> Never play small to make other women comfortable with your power.

— Inspiring Others —

You will also receive positive accolades when you show up, speak up and shine. Women who are ready to own their power will support you, and be excited for you. When one woman owns her power, she draws out the other women who are ready to own their power too. The women you inspire will propel you to keep doing your work and encourage you to keep showing up. Don't let anyone slow your roll and drive you back into your Good Girl Box. You don't belong there!

— Authenticity and Light —

When you step out of your Good Girl comfort zone, you discover what true power really is. You see that it is not about being greedy or self-centered. In fact, there is a profound goodness in true power. Embracing your power, it turns out, is about expressing your authenticity and revealing your inner light. It is about owning your value and giving other women permission to do the same.

Embracing your power is about expressing your authenticity and revealing your inner light.

Exchange the word *power* with the words *authenticity and light* and a whole new dimension of power is revealed. When you own and express your power in this way, you understand that it is a gift that you give others. Stepping into your power is an act of generosity and courage.

— Create a Powerful Sisterhood —

As you release the myth, madness and misery of playing small, you need to call in your sisterhood—your tribe of evolving soul sisters who can both support you and transport you to a new level. The more you are accepted, respected and celebrated by your sisterhood, the easier it is to DIVA UP! When we join together, there is nothing we can't achieve.

Look at the women in your life now. Do you feel seen, respected and celebrated? If not, seek out women who are a positive mirror for you. Don't settle for less. Ask yourself if you are celebrating, respecting and supporting other women as they awaken into their power? If not, start now. When you support women who are powerful, you empower yourself.

Power is contagious. Surround yourself with women who own their power and support you to do the same. Through them, you can recognize what is possible and true for you as well. Every day we choose to make our lives a playground of love and self-acceptance or a battleground of envy and comparison. We have the power to choose between them. It's our choice. Women who are ready to be empowered will support you to stand in your worth, your light and your authenticity.

Power is contagious.
Surround yourself with women
who own their power and
support you to do the same.

Do I judge or support
women who are powerful?

16

Power Play #7
Recognize Your Spiritual Good Girl

If light is in your heart, you will find your way home.

—Rumi

There is one more Good Girl that we need to visit—the Spiritual Good Girl. Spirituality and religion strike at the heart of the Good Girl's universe—*goodness*. When our Good Girl is also spiritual, she gets a double Good Girl whammy.

Your spiritual path may fit you to a tee. You may be perfectly happy with it. But after working with women for over two decades, I have seen that religion and spirituality can be another place where our Good Girl plays small, hides, abandons herself and gives her power away. In this way, the Spiritual Good Girl can be a master of self-abandonment and self-sabotage.

The Good Girl wants to be both good and spiritual, so she buys into the program and gives it her all. She is convinced she is on her way to nirvana, salvation, heaven or enlightenment if she just sacrifices a little more, adheres to the rules more diligently, or attends one more (expensive) ten-day meditation retreat. It's heaven or bust for the Spiritual Good Girl.

Power Play #7
Recognize Your Spiritual Good Girl

There are many ways our Good Girl can hijack our spirituality. In our desire for spiritual connection, we can fall in line, follow the crowd and just settle for doing what is expected of us—*conform*. But if we hope to *wake-up*, we need to be fully present for our own spiritual awakening. Spirituality and religion are intensely personal matters of the heart. I am not suggesting that you toss out your spirituality or your religious affiliation. Nor do I recommend that you blame it for your inadequacies. There are so many benefits to spirituality and religion. The suggestion here is to check in with yourself to make sure your spiritual/religious path is not disempowering you in any way. If something about it doesn't feel right, give yourself permission to make a course correction. Don't fall asleep at the wheel and let someone else take over. Trust your inner compass. It will always lead you back home.

I crawled out from underneath an ashram rock to start writing my books, but I had to believe in myself enough to do this. I had created a split between materiality and spirituality. I thought that pursuing anything in the material world meant I was ego-driven. Nothing mattered to me except my spiritual development. I had decided that money wasn't important and my own goals weren't important. As a Spiritual Good Girl, my greatest virtue was in being ego-less, which is another way of being selfless. It all played right into my Good Girl's disempowered belief system. To regain my power, I had to recognize that I was in a spiritual trap.

It was up to me to see through these lies to reclaim my balance, my truth and my power. There are endless ways we can get trapped in Spiritual Good Girl land. We can feel special, and even superior, for our unique spiritual path. Or, we may be pressured to carry on a particular tradition. We might fear that we will be shamed (or shunned) for leaving our religious affiliation.

You have your own Spiritual Good Girl story. What is it?

There are a lot of ways the Spiritual Good Girl can potentially give up her power, so it is important to pay attention. We are naturally attracted to power, but we are meant to discover it in ourselves! It is sage advice not to give up your power to any tradition, religion, guru, spiritual path, institution or organization. This includes a yoga teacher, healer, spiritual teacher or coach who you perceive is more advanced, spiritual or more powerful than you are.

The connection you have to yourself is paramount. This is where you will find the truth. Find the path that feels truly supportive and nourishing to your soul. Continue to expand into your worth and power, and make no apology for doing what is right for you.

Make no apology for doing what is right for you.

How can I expand
more into the truth of
my worth and power?

17

Power Play #8

Be Inner-Sourced

Don't let anyone stop you from loving who you are.

—Lady Gaga

Imagine you have planned to take a hot air balloon ride. You get up bright and early on a clear, crisp day excited to have an adventure. You climb into the giant basket expecting a magnificent ascension, but it doesn't happen. The problem is that you don't know how to stoke the fire to fill the balloon with hot air, and this means you can't rise and soar. Instead, you are dragged around on the ground by the whim of the wind (the whim of others.) This is what it feels like to give your power away—people can drag you around.

You might imagine a woman who gives her power away falls under the spell of a domineering person and can't keep her boundaries. But this is just one example. It is easy to recognize how other people give their power away, but it isn't easy to see how we give our power away. Knowing your Good Girl Type gives you vital clues, but you still need to be vigilant in observing your patterns. The more you look, the more you will see.

Even confident and self-aware women can give their power away. For example, we could be in our sovereignty at work, but at home we spoil our children and enable their bad behavior. This is a form of people-pleasing. Whenever we don't create and maintain our boundaries, we give our power away. Whenever we betray our own best interests, we give our power away. And, when we abandon our truth, we give our power away.

Whenever we don't create and maintain our boundaries, we give our power away.

This doesn't mean you need to always *get your way!* Compromise in relationships is necessary, but betraying ourselves is not. We give our power away when we abandon ourselves. This occurs when we fail to:

- *Do what is best for ourselves*

- *Consider our own needs and well-being*

- *Make and keep boundaries that matter to us*

- *Speak our truth*

- *Say "No" when we want to (and need to)*

A healthy relationship should support you in doing all of these things. No relationship should ask you to give your power away. For example, if you don't have a full voice in your relationship, you are abandoning yourself and giving your power away to the other person. Over time, you become smaller and smaller and the other person takes over.

Power Play #8
Be Inner-Sourced

Looking outside yourself for validation is another way you give your power away. The secret to reclaiming your power is to fuel yourself from within—to be inner-sourced. When you do this, you move from being powerless to powerful and from unworthy to worthy. You don't blame people for your problems, or ask them to solve them. You take responsibility for your life. When you no longer need others to validate your worth, you become an authentically empowered woman.

> When you no longer need others to validate your worth, you become an authentically empowered woman.

When your Diva is by your side, your worth and power are no longer negotiable. On one hand, it is natural and healthy to seek love, validation and approval from others. It creates a positive feedback loop that is essential to our well-being on every level. The people we choose to have in our lives should be our soft place to land. We should not have to work for their love.

However, surrounding ourselves with loving people does not get us out of the responsibility of loving and accepting ourselves. If we insist that others continually fill our empty cup, we become needy and desperate which is exhausting for those around us. We can end up blaming people for not supplying us with the love and validation we so desperately need. In this way, we create imbalances in all our relationships.

If you harbor the idea that you are unlovable, it will keep showing up in your life over and over again. Your beliefs are boomerangs. Every relationship you have ends up becoming verifiable proof that you are indeed unlovable, because you create it that way. This is how your core beliefs drive your life. When your Good Girl is no longer dedicated to shrinking and hiding, you can discard outdated beliefs and misperceptions about yourself. You can then fill up on the good stuff—your worth and power.

Your beliefs are boomerangs.

— Create Your Love-ability Basecamp —

Power happens from the inside out. It is when you know the truth of your own love-ability. The Good Girl has endless amount of love and compassion for others, but she can beat herself up mercilessly. She never feels good enough. The solution is to create your own love-ability basecamp where you know you are love, you are loving and you are lovable! Even if you think you have a strong sense of self-worth, many of us are secretly plagued with self-doubt. We fear we are not lovable as we are, and we can become obsessed with changing ourselves. We imagine that a better nose, a better body, a better bank account, a better relationship, a better career or some better *thing* can replace our own self-acceptance. This, of course, never works. The ultimate self-care is to stop believing in your own inadequacy.

It is useless to make other people responsible for your self-worth. They don't know their own value, so how could they possibly know your value? When you accept your inherent worth, everything changes. You can even dare to be indifferent to the judgments and opinions of others. Your Diva knows that no one can give you your self-worth or take it away—only you can do that.

To own your power, create a *love-ability basecamp*. Begin by loving and accepting yourself as you are. It is like having a magic wand. Without it nothing works. With it, anything is possible.

The ultimate self-care is to stop believing in your own inadequacy.

What would change
in your life if you knew
you were worthy?

18

You Are A Sovereign Queen

(So Stop Pretending You're Not!)

*I know that yes, I am powerful. I am more powerful
than my mind can even digest and understand.*

—Beyoncé

You have been on a journey into the heart of your feminine power to reclaim your sovereignty. You now know you are far from unworthy. The truth is, you are a miracle—a glittering ball of stardust here for a short road trip across time and space. Let go of all the illusions you have built up about who you *should be*—including all the judgments and assessments of your worth and power. You don't need them anymore. You don't have to prove your worth, get the approval of others, be perfect or fit the mold that others create. It's time to come out of your Good Girl Box.

There is no time for playing small or believing you are small. Your full priestess presence is requested at the table of life. When you play small, think small and believe you are small, the whole world suffers.

Your full priestess presence is requested at the table of life.

If you listen, you will hear the sound of your own inner glass ceiling breaking. Your Good Girl is no longer in the driver's seat of your life, convertible top down, blaring music and driving you off a cliff. Your Diva is your fabulous new BFF and co-pilot. Watch out world!

As you ascend above your own self-imposed limitations, you will see the big picture and know the big truth about yourself—you've always been worthy and powerful. You no longer need to worry about being good or perfect. You simply need to be true to yourself. You now have the secrets to crack your Good Girl code, own your power and create a life you love.

When I finished writing this book, I was excited to check in with my inner Diva.

Did I cover everything? Was anything left to say?

As soon as I began my guided imagery process to connect with her, she appeared in my mind's eye. She showed up in a magnificent billowy red dress and she had a big smile on her face. She reminded me of how far I have come in reclaiming my power. I was no longer Wallflower Wanda or Fix-It Fran.

My journey to reclaim my power meant rebooting my Good Girl programming from the ground up. I left behind the belief that *I didn't matter*, the thought that *small is better* and my split between materiality and spirituality. One by one, I tossed out my disempowering Good Girl beliefs and made my Diva my new BFF. In this process, I reclaimed my power, my freedom and my sovereignty.

I asked my Diva if there was anything she would like to add to the book. *"Now is your chance,"* I said.

My Diva replied, *"Life isn't about following the rules, it is about staying true to yourself no matter what. Get in tune with your holy truth and live by it. This is what it means to reclaim your power."*

Get in tune with your holy truth and live by it.

My Diva concluded by saying, *"Be big, be bold, wear red, stand out, speak up, show up and shine bright. And never be afraid to speak the truth or break the rules."*

Through the 4 Good Girl Types and the 8 Power Plays, you have learned that honoring yourself is not selfish. It is respectful. Doing what is right for you does not mean you are uncaring. It means you care for yourself as well as others. When you crack your Good Girl code, you become free to let your authentic self shine through. Creating a life that works for you requires that you break your own rules, as well as the rules imposed upon you. The glass ceiling is inside us, as much as it is outside of us.

The glass ceiling is inside us, as much as it is outside of us.

This is just the beginning. You have already dismantled the lies and ties that keep you in your Good Girl Box. You now know you are both good and powerful. You can express both compassion and strength and be both feminine and strong. There is no reason to hide your worth or power. All that is left to do is pick up your scepter, straighten your crown and *own* it!

Shine on! I am right there with you.

Be big, be bold, wear red,
stand out, speak up,
show up and shine bright.

Never be afraid to speak the
truth or break the rules.

The Diva-tudes

Don't apologize for:

Your point of view
Your opinions
Your decisions
Your truth
Your power
Your talent
Your beauty
Your sexuality
Your body
Your ambition
Your strength

Stand up to people who:

Silence you
Control you
Use you
Shame you
Discourage you
Judge you

Decide:

What is right for you
What is true for you
What you want

Move toward:

What uplifts you
What inspires you
What motivates you

Don't hide:

Your truth
Your power
Your worth
Your dreams

Recognize how:

You give up your power
You play small
You betray yourself

Stand up for:

What you want
What you believe in
What is true for you

Know that:

You are love.
You are loving.
You are lovable.

The Daily Diva Check-In

4 Questions to Empower Your Day

What would NOURISH my HEART & SOUL today?

What ATTITUDE would support me powerfully today?

*What ACTIONS would move me closer
to achieving my goals?*

What BELIEF is no longer serving me?

Joy Balma, MA, MS is a bestselling author, women's power mentor and personality type expert. She has Master's degrees in both psychology and Oriental medicine. After owning a women's wellness center for fifteen years, she realized women needed a way to see their patterns clearly. Joy created The Feminine Type Success System™ which she shared in her first book, *Rock Your Feminine Type To Rock Your Business.*

In *Crack Your Good Girl Code,* Joy helps women heal their disempowered Good Girl and reclaim their power so they can create a life they love.

For more information on Joy's
books, trainings and retreats,
visit
www.JoyBalma.com